REASON IN HISTORY

The Library of Liberal Arts
OSKAR PIEST, FOUNDER

REASON
IN HISTORY

*A General Introduction to
the Philosophy of History*

G. W. F. HEGEL

Translated, with an introduction, by
ROBERT S. HARTMAN

The Library of Liberal Arts
published by
THE BOBBS-MERRILL COMPANY, INC.
INDIANAPOLIS · NEW YORK

Georg Wilhelm Friedrich Hegel: 1770-1831

LECTURES ON THE PHILOSOPHY OF HISTORY was

originally published in 1837

. . . .

PREFACE

The translation of a philosophical classic into a modern language is a difficult task, no matter how clear the original. If the original itself is not very clear, the difficulties increase. But if, as in our case, the original was never written, but narrated —by a notoriously bad lecturer—and taken down by his, mostly lay, students, the task of translation becomes truly hazardous— as is evidenced by previous English renderings of this text.

The German original is not only often ambiguous and obscure, but the style is extremely uneven. It continually oscillates between the stilted and the colloquial, no doubt because of the manner of its composition. Hegel often reaches either too high or too low, and there is little effort to focus the word exactly on the thought. The importance of Sibree's pioneer translation, which I have consulted and followed in some places, is not to be minimized. Sibree, however, consistently takes the high road; he is complex even where Hegel is simple. I have chosen the opposite approach. In steering between the conservatism of literal translation and the radicalism of transliteration, I have taken a middle course, slightly right of center. Sibree's translation has been called baroque; the present translation, by comparison, might be called Georgian. Although it is more complete and, it is hoped, more correct than previous ones, it is by no means a definitive translation. This, I am persuaded, would have to be a paraphrase of the original.

That, in spite of its risks, the translation was undertaken is due primarily to the editor of The Library of Liberal Arts, Mr. Oskar Piest, whose cooperation, constructive criticism, and relentless drive for perfection were a continuous source of encouragement. My special thanks are due to Professor Paul Schrecker of the University of Pennsylvania, who critically examined the entire manuscript, clarified many of the obscurities of the text, and made numerous suggestions which improved both the accuracy and style of the translation.

The merits of this translation are in large part due to the help I have received. Its shortcomings are entirely my own.

ROBERT S. HARTMAN

CONTENTS

· · · · · · · · · · · · · · · · ·

REASON IN HISTORY

INTRODUCTION

I. THE SIGNIFICANCE OF HEGEL FOR HISTORY

In Hegel, philosophy and history met. He was the outstanding philosopher of history, as well as historian of philosophy.
But more than that, he was the one philosopher who deci-
sively changed history. Philosophers before him have had a
hand in history, both as persons and as bearers of ideas—Plato,
Hobbes, Leibniz, Locke, Rousseau—but, as Ernst Cassirer re-
marks, "no other philosophical system has exerted such a
strong and enduring influence upon political life as the metaphysics of Hegel. . . . There has hardly been a single great
political system that has resisted its influence." [1] All recent
political ideologies bear his stamp. Just as in Hegel's philosophy the "Idea," the logical power of the divine, enters and
guides, through mortal men, the scene of historical struggle,
so has Hegel's philosophy itself, as an expression of the absolute Idea, entered history. And just as the Idea remains untouched by the struggle of human passions [2] which actualize it,
so Hegel's philosophy stands unconcerned, as an intellectual
creation, above the mortal struggle that has been and is being
fought in its name. Some men have drawn this philosophy
into the strife of parties and attacked its cool and remote
author as a villain and his philosophy as a psychotic product.
They confuse Hegel's philosophy with the often hysteric
use that has been made of it. The philosophical arguments to
which Hegel gave rise have, as Cassirer rightly says,

. . . become a mortal combat. A historian recently raised the
question whether the struggle of the Russians and the invad-
ing Germans in 1943 was not, at bottom, a conflict between
the Left and the Right wings of Hegel's school. That may
seem to be an exaggerated statement of the problem but it
contains a nucleus of truth.[3]

[1] *The Myth of the State,* New Haven, Yale University Press, 1946, p. 248.
[2] See below, pp. 43f.
[3] Cassirer, *op. cit.,* p. 249.

We may find the manifold influences of Hegel's philosophy foreshadowed in the historical constellation in the year of his birth, 1770. That year Marie Antoinette, the radiant Archduchess of Austria, was married to the dull Dauphin of France. At Ajaccio, Napoleon, the second son of Laetizia Buonaparte, was just learning to walk. Captain Cook was completing his first trip around the world. At Boston, Massachusetts, some English soldiers fired into a crowd of colonials. At Königsberg, Germany, an overaged *Privatdozent*, named Immanuel Kant, read a dissertation concerning form and principles of the sensible and intelligible worlds and man's position between the two. At the opposite end of Germany, at Strasbourg, a young student, Goethe, wrote some poems which swept the whole of Germany into his own sensuous love for Friederike of Sesenheim. A little later the novel of his second love, *The Sufferings of Young Werther*, swept the whole world, as far as China, into a wave of romantic suicides. In France, that same year, Baron of Holbach published a treatise showing that the world, far from being a romantic place, was nothing but a large clockwork. When Hegel died, in 1831, the beheaded body of Marie Antoinette lay in a common grave at Paris. Both Napoleon and the Revolution had run their course. The great man had been taken care of by the English and the Revolution by Metternich. The American Republic had taken her place among the powers, and her fast clippers roamed the Seven Seas. Goethe serenely surveyed a life of a thousand conflicts merged into classic form and sealed his epic of Faust, the universal man, who transcends the world of sensuousness. Holbach was out of fashion; but a thirteen-year-old boy at Trier, Karl Marx, born the year that Hegel became professor of philosophy at the University of Berlin, was already discovering philosophy—which meant Hegel—and would soon resurrect Holbach in a form more dynamic than all romanticism and which would sweep the world, as far as China, with a passion of the intellect more powerful than anything that Werther knew.

In both, the triumph of romanticism—in philosophy as well

as politics—and that of intellectualism, Hegel played a decisive role. The influence of his philosophy confirms his thesis that universal Reason, through men, shapes history. The fate of this philosophy bears witness to its dialectic form. The most rational and religious philosopher, Hegel unchained the most irrational and irreligious movements—Fascism and Communism. Often regarded as the most authoritarian, he inspired the most democratic: Walt Whitman and John Dewey. The philosopher who equated what is with what ought to be, he released the greatest dissatisfaction with what is; and thus, as the greatest conservative, unchained the greatest revolution. The form of his philosophy battled with its content, and the content with its form. They separated. Some thinkers accepted the content of his philosophy and opposed its form. They became conservatives and so-called "Hegelians of the Right." Other thinkers accepted the form of his philosophy and opposed its content. They became revolutionaries and "Hegelians of the Left." The two opposing factions met finally in the mortal embrace of Stalingrad.

What won at Stalingrad was the revolutionary form, not the conservative content of Hegel's philosophy. This concrete fact corresponds to the abstract situation. The power of Hegel's philosophy lies in its form rather than its content. Although the content is overwhelming in its encyclopedic width, yet the transitions from fact to fact, following the links of the dialectic concatenation, are sometimes forced, and the "facts" marshaled little factual. On the other hand, what brilliance and perspicacity the philosophy has, and the very universality of its scope, it owes to the method—the dialectic logic—which drove Hegel on and on to encompass more and more phenomena, wider and wider regions of knowledge, within its systematic frame. The secret, then, of Hegel's influence is his dynamic method. This he did not invent; its roots go back to the very sources of Greek philosophy, in Heraclitus; and a thread can be traced, and has been traced by Hegel, throughout the history of philosophy. But he elaborated and applied it to the totality of the world and its equipment. The power of the method lies in its inner dynamic and universal applicability. One thought, in an almost literal sense, "gives" the next—thesis leading to antithesis, and both to synthesis, the latter serving as new thesis for another train of thought encompassing the first, and so on *ad infinitum*—until the whole world and all things in it are caught in the chain of dialectic. This is possible, on the one hand, through the complete formalism of the method, that is, its independence from any concrete fact; and, on the other hand, its complete immersion in the concrete factuality of the world. Hegel treated pure thought both as *pure* and as *thought,* that is, both as ideal reality "before the creation of the world," distinct from all existence; yet, once there is an existent world, as arising out of and being part of it. Thought is what is ideal in the world; the world is what is concrete in the Idea. For the Idea is not static but dynamic; it gives rise, by its own inner dynamic, to all that exists. All existence is the manifestation, the actualization, of the Idea. Only by being actualized does the Idea receive its full reality, and only by containing the Idea does the existing obtain its full existence. Thus, reality becomes more real in existence, and existence more existent in reality. Thought and thing merge, and each becomes more what it is by being the other.

All this is not as difficult and obscure as it sounds, once the underlying dialectic dynamic of the Idea and its rôle in history are understood. The Idea develops both in space and in time. The Idea developing in space is Nature, the Idea subsequently —or rather consequently, for it is all a *logical* process—developing in time is Spirit. The latter, the development of the Idea in time, or of Spirit, is History. History thus becomes one of the great movements of the Idea; it becomes embedded in a metaphysical flow of universal scope. It is universal History. At the same time, since the universal process is logical, it becomes systematic, or, as Hegel says,[4] scientific history.

The Hegelian system has interpreted and touched all the great historical and spiritual events of and since his time. The

[4] See below, pp. 12, 24.

cruelties of the French Revolution were interpreted by Hegel as logical abstractions run wild: the vagueness and abstractness of Rousseau's General Will superimposed without analysis upon a concrete particular situation. Later, when German students again raised the flag of revolution—much less violently to be sure, but again pursuing vague and undefined aims—the Prussian Minister of Education, von Allenstein, called Hegel to Berlin to cure the political immaturity of the young men by a philosophy which would patiently explain the evolution of social and political realities. Not only students but also officers and officials listened to his lectures, and for more than a decade he was what some have called the Royal Prussian Court Philosopher. This does not speak against Hegel but rather for the Prussian state. For what state, before or since, has thought to find the cure for its political ills in the teaching of a philosopher, recognized as the greatest of his time in spirit, independence, and integrity, and subsidized him for quiet production, content to follow rather than to command him? Thus, while Hegel became the father of the revolution of the twentieth century, he pacified that of the nineteenth. For this he has often been called a reactionary, and reaction he did help. But, as the readers of this text will find, the state that the reactionaries preserved was not the State which for Hegel was the culmination of world history. Here is one of the many misunderstandings to which Hegel's philosophy gave rise, not only through its inherent dialectic but also, it must be said, through its often careless presentation.

Similar misunderstandings adhere to the notion of the "great man," whom Hegel was the first to discuss philosophically. Like Nietzsche's superman, the Hegelian hero was misunderstood and mistakenly regarded as prototype for the subhuman man of Fascism and Nazism. But Hegel fathered these movements in a much more subtle way. When writing of the great man, he was thinking of Napoleon. What he has to say about him is true even though it describes only one aspect of the phenomenon of the world-historical person. If history is, as he holds, the self-development of Spirit, the actualization of the divine Idea, of a cosmic plan, then the historical man must be one in whom the potentialities of the time, the historical situation, concentrate themselves. But he is only a phase in the great world process, connected with individual states. At the end of the historical process, when the Spirit has fully realized itself, stands a global state of universal Reason, of all mankind. In it the absolute Idea would be fulfilled, and historical and spiritual greatness coincide. Hegel is not specific on this, and some of his interpreters have held that the world was for him to be forever a battlefield of states. But what Hegel did not express clearly himself he found expressed in Wilhelm von Humboldt's words which serve as a motto before the "Lectures on the Philosophy of History": "World history is incomprehensible without world government."

Certain it is that for Hegel history did not close with the Prussian state, as has often been held. Those readers of the "Lectures on the Philosophy of History" who follow them to the end will find that he saw in America "the land of the future." The present state of history, that of his time, was for him the relative, not the absolute end of the world-historical process. At the end of the "Lectures" we find the statement: "To this point consciousness has come." What he means is that the self-development of Consciousness has come to the point of Hegel's present. The Prussian state of his time is the highest development of history—relatively, not absolutely. In it Spirit has actualized itself most fully *thus far*. But this concrete existence of Spirit is by no means the absolute reality of Spirit. Here again, the reason that Hegel's meaning has so often been misunderstood lies in the presentation of his philosophy, which indeed is often unclear and sometimes careless —as if Hegel, in the onrush of thoughts and the tremendous output of a relatively short life, had had no time to polish his work with care. This is also true of the "Lectures," which in their present form were not written by Hegel but were edited on the basis of students' lecture notes.

The spirit of Hegel's philosophy is less authoritarian than it is often represented. It is true, from his works, especially when misunderstood, a case for his authoritarian views can be made. But from the same works a case can be made for the opposite views.

It is a historical fact that Hegel greatly influenced the man who became the prophet of American democracy, Walt Whitman. Whitman, like Hegel, sees the state as a cultural unit; as the totality of all the artistic, economic, political, and moral ideas and institutions of the people. Like Hegel, he recognizes the "principle" of a people, its own unique spirit; like him he sees the unbroken chain of generations combining to the wholeness of history beyond and above the will of the individual, and indeed beyond the terrestrial globe:

Within the purposes of the Cosmos, and vivifying all meteorology, and all the congeries of the mineral, the vegetable and animal worlds—all the physical growth and development of man, and all the history of the race in politics, religions, wars, etc., there is a moral purpose, a visible or invisible intention, certainly underlying all. . . . That something is the All, and the idea of All, with the accompanying idea of eternity, and of itself, the soul, buoyant, indestructible, sailing space forever.[5]

This is the poetic version of the Hegelian vision. And Whitman knows that his dream is Hegelian. The poet of the future, who is to sing and incarnate the coming total democracy, must sing the Hegelian harmony:

In the future of these States must arise poets immenser far . . . poets not only possessed of the religious fire and abandon of Isaiah, luxurious in the epic talent of Homer, or for proud characters in Shakespeare, but consistent with the Hegelian formulas.[6]

Thus Hegel has inspired not only totalitarians of Right and Left but also the poet of democracy. As he has inspired America's poet, so he has inspired America's philosopher. Dewey's

[5] Walt Whitman, *Democratic Vistas*, The Little Library of Liberal Arts, pp. 62f.

[6] *Ibid.*, p. 63.

early philosophy is a translation of Hegel's method into experiential and, Dewey thought, modern scientific terms. In the process of translation the old text has all but disappeared. But many of its principles remain. The fusion of thought and its object, the dynamic of logical thought, the progress of thinking from the indeterminate to the determinate, the necessity of thought for human life—all these are Hegelian elements in John Dewey. Also, the encyclopedic scope of Dewey's philosophy and his effectiveness within American civilization remind one of Hegel's similar stature in his time and environment.

On Kant, of course, Hegel had no influence, but his influence was profound on Kantian philosophy. Hegel rejects Kant's program of examining the faculty of understanding before examining the nature of things. For him things and thought are dialectically interrelated. Hegel compared Kant's program with that of the scholastic who wanted to learn to swim before he ventured into the water. Thought, for Hegel, recognizes things themselves. There is no thing "in itself," lying unknowably beyond thought, not even God. On the contrary, as we read in our text, we not only have the possibility, we have the duty of knowing Him.[7] For if the laws of logic and those of reality belong together as two aspects of the same process, then logic is at the same time a doctrine of reality, or ontology. And the principles of logic, or categories, are at the same time those of reality. The logical categories are the laws of the world, and the laws of the world are the logical categories. Arrived at this point, Hegel needed to take but one step to regard reality itself as the thought of a *thinker,* and the whole system of the world as a theology. The divine thinker thinks the world; his thought is at the same time the world and the process of his thinking the world process. The laws of logic as those of the divine mind are Reason. Since they are at the same time those of the world, all that is real is rational and all that is rational is real. Also, since the divine thought progresses according to its own laws, which are the

[7] See below, p. 16.

laws of the world, all that is must be and all is as it ought to be. But what is real in existence is only that which is divine in it. Only this it is which develops. Everything else is contingent and must perish. The interrelationship between the real and the merely existent, the necessary and the contingent, proceeds dialectically: thesis and antithesis contradict each other, and the synthesis preserves and continues what is worthwhile and necessary in both. The dialectic process is thus at the same time logical, ontological, and chronological. All that happens in the world has not only temporal but also logical and ontological significance. The temporal is but an aspect of the eternal and of its ontological structure. On the other hand, actualization in the world does something to the eternal Idea. Man's spirit, the synthesis of the divine Idea and Nature, makes the indeterminate reality of the Idea determinate in existence. Thus, in thinking more and more about the world and, in the process, developing his own consciousness more and more, he makes the Idea, that is, the divine thinker Himself, more and more conscious of Himself. All this goes on in the course of human generations, organized in states and nations, that is, in History. History, thus, is the progressing self-determination of the Idea, the progressing self-development of Spirit. In addition, since Spirit by its inner nature is free, History is the progress of Freedom.

Into this somewhat complicated scheme Hegel inserts the facts of history. The main fact, which seems to confirm his thesis, is that in past Oriental civilizations *one* was free; in classical antiquity, Greece and Rome, *some* were free; and in modern Germanic and Anglo-Saxon civilizations, *all* are free. He thus constructs world history by using the logical quantifiers; fortunately they form a triad suitable for dialectic treatment. But the neat scheme does not quite agree with historical reality, and for this reason the "Lectures on the Philosophy of History" are seldom read today in their entirety. Yet, the thesis, presented in the Introduction, is fundamentally sound: that history is the progress of freedom. This Hegelian thesis is nothing new. It was actually stated by Kant long before it was stated by Hegel. But Hegel gave it the grander, indeed, the universal setting. Therefore his philosophy of history has had incomparably deeper influence than Kant's. Hegel simply caught more of history's spirit. For Kant it is not God but Nature that has designs for men in history. Her cunning uses not the great man or the great historical passion but all the small passions within us. By them she goads us on to find a mode of living together peacefully in society. Society is the gradual result of the antagonism between our individual and our social inclinations. Thus freedom in society is for Kant a product of Nature and history, "progress in the consciousness of freedom." This is precisely Hegel's formulation. It appeared in Kant's essay [8] when Hegel was fourteen years old— as old as Karl Marx was when Hegel died. In Kant's definition, "freedom," "progress," and "consciousness" have a more pedestrian meaning. When Hegel took over, the spirit of history began to blow through philosophy.

Therefore Kant's work never inspired the young and romantic people as did Hegel's. In the encyclopedic mood of Hegel, the romantic found a kindred soul—sweeping the whole world, God and man, Nature and Spirit, into one cosmic feeling, one *Weltgefühl*. Hegel's rationality was the result of such a feeling. His purpose and program, his sweep and vision, the boldness of his conception, are unlimited. Even in our text romantic passages occur, when Hegel is carried away by the splendor of his own visions, the "glory and majesty" of Reason, and the grandeur of the historical spectacle. The cosmic unity of the world in all its manifestations is of course the heart of Hegel's conception. He finds in feeling the beginning of Reason, in the first ripples of emotion the latent intellect, and in sense perception the traces of Spirit.[9] Though Hegel was the most sober of the three Tübingen student friends—the other two, Schelling and Hölderlin, called him

---

[8] *Ideen zu einer allgemeinen Geschichte in weltbürgerlicher Absicht* ("Ideas Concerning a Universal History in Cosmopolitan Spirit"), 1784.

[9] See below, pp. 17ff., 67. Hegel anticipates here a thesis developed in our time by Ernst Cassirer.

the "old man"—his is a sobriety which to any philistine would seem drunkenness.

It is not his influence on romanticism, however, but on materialism which has given him his historical significance. It is paradoxical, and quite in keeping with Hegel's dialectic of history, that the most idealistic philosopher, who even tried to make the realm of dead nature into one of ideal dynamics, should be the father, or rather the grandfather, of the most belligerently materialistic philosophy. Although Hegel was unsuccessful as a natural philosopher, he was uniquely successful as a social philosopher. The reason is that the logic of the natural sciences had been worked out successfully long before Hegel's time by the mathematical philosophers of the Renaissance, whereas for the social sciences, or for moral philosophy, no comparable logical tool was at hand. Even today Hegel's is the most elaborate intellectual tool of social analysis, which may partly account for the intellectual success of Marxism. All non-Hegelian social scientists are in comparison handicapped and—through lack of an equally systematic tool—confined to either empirical descriptions or lesser generalizations.

As Hegel conceived his method, it was to be "a science of pure thought" which, in the words of a modern writer, was "to develop an unprecedented political philosophy . . . like geometry in its coherence, in which human philosophical thought would reach systematic expression." [10] Just as an astronomer must know the laws of mathematics and geometry in order to apply them to the stars, so the historian must know the dialectic of the Idea in order to apply it to history. Thus, in our text,[11] the mathematical method, applied to natural phenomena, is compared to the dialectic method, applied to social phenomena.

It is Hegel's dialectic method, in its Marxian secularization —that is, the "sloughing off" of its idealistic content—on which the Marxists base their claim of "scientific" procedure. Yet the dialectic method is "scientific" only in comparison with

[10] Catlin, *Story of the Political Philosophers*, New York, 1939, p. 490.
[11] See below, p. 79.

the relatively unscientific status of the social sciences. Compared with the scientific method in the natural sciences it, too, is unscientific.

The difference between Hegelian idealism and Marxian materialism, and the rise of the latter out of the former, is a story too complex to be told here. Suffice it to say that, historically seen, Hegel's work is the intermediary between Holbach and Marx. It enabled Marx to formulate materialism as a "scientific" system, which is to Holbach's generalities as chemistry is to alchemy and which made materialism into a doctrine applicable, like a science, to all phases of social and political life.

For Marx as for Hegel—and also for Kant—history is an impersonal process. The historical person is for him, as for Hegel, only the exponent of historical forces: he does not *make* history, he executes it. For Hegel the driving power of history is the dynamic of the Idea; for Marx it is the dynamic of economic development, dialectically giving rise to a series of classes which struggle for possession of the state. Thus Marx took from Hegel the idea of process, the idea of progress (the teleological course of history), the dialectic method, the suprapersonal power of history, the primacy of the collective over the individual, the lack of personal ethics. He rejected the theological, metaphysical, and what ethical content the system has, its panpsychic tendencies, the identity of logic and being; and he translated the dialectic into a principle of economic and political revolution. He applied the dialectic to one aspect of reality, whereas Hegel tried to apply it to all aspects, intertwining religion and metaphysics, psychology and value, being and time, both with his logic and with one another. Karl Marx, on the other hand, crystallized one aspect of the world. He thus brought the Hegelian method into sharp focus and gave it acuteness and striking power. Yet, he himself, and still more his followers, fell in turn for the Hegelian temptation of universality. In universalizing a limited field into a new system of the world they became dogmatic and megalomaniac. In getting rid of some of the metaphysical "trimmings" of the Hegelian system they also got rid of some of the fundamental truths of human existence, especially Freedom.

II. THE SIGNIFICANCE OF HISTORY
FOR HEGEL

1. IDEA AND SPIRIT

History, *for Hegel, is the development of Spirit in Time, just as Nature is the development of the Idea in Space.*[12] If we understand this sentence we understand Hegel's philosophy of history. Hegel's whole system is built on the great triad: Idea—Nature—Spirit. The Idea-in-itself is that which develops, the dynamic reality of and behind—or before—the world. Its antithesis, Idea-outside-of-itself, namely Space, is Nature. Nature develops, after the stages of the mineral and vegetable kingdom, into man, in whose consciousness the Idea becomes conscious of itself. This self-consciousness of the Idea is Spirit, the antithesis of Idea and Nature, and the development of this consciousness is History. History and the Idea, thus, are interrelated. The Idea is the nature of God's will, and since this Idea becomes truly itself only in and through History, History is, as a modern writer has well characterized it, "the autobiography of God." [13] Or, in the words of another modern writer,[14] God for Hegel not only *has* but *is* History. History, for Hegel, is not the appearance, it is the reality of God. For him it is not nature that is divine, as it was for Spinoza, but History. The Spinozistic formula *Deus sive natura* becomes the Hegelian formula *Deus sive historia.*[15] God and world belong together; without the world God would

[12] See below, pp. 20, 87.

[13] Sidney Hook, *From Hegel to Marx,* New York, Humanities Press, 1950, p. 36.

[14] Cassirer, *The Myth of the State,* p. 262.

[15] *Ibid.*

not be God.[16] The Idea-in-itself is only the starting point of God—God before Creation. Creation itself completes God. In Creation, then, God can be known. To bring about the knowledge of God through an understanding of the world's history is the task of philosophy, and, in particular, of the philosophy of history. Thus philosophy is the divine Idea, or Reason, in the process of knowing itself. In addition to this epistemological mission, philosophy also has an ethical mission. In seeing in History the actualization, the unfolding of the divine plan, and supposing, as a matter of definition, that God is good, this view of history is necessarily optimistic. The dread of accident is overcome in the disregard of contingency. Only the good is necessary and will prevail. What perishes was not worth its existence, except as a step to the good. History thus is the justification of God and His goodness; it is Theodicy.[17]

What Hegel means by the "Time" in which History develops is a problem which he fails to discuss in our text. He mentions it in *Phenomenology of Mind*. It is not physical time, for this, together with Space, belongs in the Hegelian system to Nature. The "Space" in which Nature develops is physical space-time. The Time in which Spirit develops is the time of consciousness, in which Spirit "empties and externalizes" itself and in which Spirit beats out the "phases" of history. As the Idea-in-itself develops in the pureness of logical dialectic, so the Idea-outside-itself, as Nature, develops in the form of Space. And Spirit—the Idea-in-and-for-itself—develops in the form of Time, the Spirit's Time of consciousness. Time, then, is to Spirit what logical structure is to the Idea. It is the concrete counterpart of Logic in the realm of Spirit, just as is space-time in the realm of Nature. The science of the Idea is that of logical structure, namely, logic; the science of Nature is that of Space, namely, geometry; [18] the

---

[16] Hegel, *Philosophy of Religion*, 1895, I, p. 200.

[17] See below, p. 18.

[18] Hegel did not draw this possible consequence of his theory. Only modern physical science has done so.

science of Spirit is that of Time, namely, history. The mutual relations can be seen in the following table:

	Thesis	Antithesis	Synthesis
	Idea	Nature	Spirit
Structure:	Dialectic (Logical Dynamic)	Space-Time	Time
Science:	Logic	Geometry	History

It is seen that the philosophy of history is the culmination of the Hegelian system. History is the complete concretion of logic, which is the basis of the system. Since Spirit is concrete Idea, the sequence of historical events is both temporal and logical; it is temporal in so far as it is the self-development of Spirit, and it is logical in so far as it is the self-development of the Idea. As such it is consequence. For the idealistic philosopher, the self-development of the Spirit transforms the primary logical consequence into temporal sequence. For the historian, on the other hand, for whom temporal sequence is primary, the self-development of the Idea transforms this temporal sequence into logical consequence. Again, since the logical differentiation of the Idea becomes in the course of its further differentiations temporal, Time is simply another dimension—after logical structure and space—of the development of the Idea. Temporal process is simply another kind of process following dialectically after the logical process, which is the essential process of the Idea-in-itself, and the spatial, which is the essential process of the Idea-outside-of-itself, or Nature. Again, since Spirit is the synthesis of Idea and Nature, Time is the corresponding synthesis of logical structure and Space. From this point of view we may call Time logicized Space or spatialized logical dynamic,[19] where logical dynamic and Space

[19] The spatial nature of Time logically apprehended has been discussed by Bergson.

are antitheses. That is to say, wherever Space is to be dynamic, it must be so in Time. Thus history, as Hegel makes clear, is both in Space and in Time; it occurs in Nature as well as in Mind. Since history is the result of the dynamic of the divine Idea, this Idea is creative of all that is in history. What the medieval philosophers ascribed to the mystery of God—that His thought is creation of things—Hegel ascribes to the logical system which is the essence of God. Without this actualization, as we have seen, the Idea itself is not real, just as no thing has full existence without the ideal in it. This means, logically, that the universal fulfills itself in the particular and the particular in the universal. This doctrine of the concrete universal is in our text applied to the relationship between Spirit or Universal History and the human individual, in and through which Spirit becomes concrete. While individuals are mortal, Spirit is eternal. The tension between the transitoriness of individual life and the eternity of history, between Spirit and its own historical phases, constitutes the dialectic of history.

Spirit does not disappear when the life that carries it disappears. The great show of history goes on. What perishes is the mere existence of the present. The reality of the present, that is, the present which has manifested the Idea, appears sublimated in the future. Spirit gains the consciousness of its own past, "of that which it was," [20] and thus reappears after each disappearance of the particular stage, in a new particular stage which includes the thoughts of the previous one. Thus, as it says at the end of our text, "the moments which Spirit seems to have left behind, it still possesses in the depth of its present." In the decay of the particular phases Spirit gains its universality. With every passing phase, thought is enriched about the past. Indeed, the past as element of the Spirit is possible only by the passing of concrete actuality; the passing of actuality is the condition for the ever-progressing life of Spirit. Thus the historical process is for Hegel the continuous disappearance of the ideally negative; or positively expressed,

[20] See below, p. 94.

it is the ever clearer self-presentation and self-representation of Spirit.

Thus the more happens in history, the more Spirit can develop itself, can know and think. Only stagnation would be inimical to history. Yet the happening must not be blind, chaotic, undirected. Spirit is not enriched by merely grasping the concrete in its passing. Rather, some events are more and some are less in accord with it. Spirit not only is dynamic, has a rate of progress, is, as we may say, quantitative; it also has a quality, a goal, a direction: that actuality will last longest and prevail within the chaos of events whose quality most closely resembles that of Spirit itself. This quality, as was mentioned before, is Freedom.

2. FREEDOM

That Spirit is Freedom Hegel shows in our text in three ways. Man is part Nature and part Spirit, but his essence is Spirit. The more man develops spiritually, the more he becomes conscious of himself; and the more he becomes conscious of himself, the more he becomes himself, that is, free. Thus the development of Spirit toward consciousness of itself in world history is the development to ever purer Freedom. World history is the progress of Freedom, because it is the progress of the self-consciousness of Spirit. Thus, secondly, not only man becomes free, but Spirit itself, in and through man. Spirit is essentially reflective; it makes for itself necessarily a certain idea of itself, of its own nature. Thus it arrives at a content of its reflection, not by *finding* a content, but rather by *"making itself* into its own object, its own content. Knowledge is its form and conduct. The content of knowledge, however, is the spiritual itself. Thus Spirit is essentially with itself, that is, free." [21] That Spirit is Freedom is seen, thirdly, not in the nature of man nor of Spirit, but in that of its opposite, namely, Matter. Matter is heavy because, in gravitation, each piece of Matter strives toward something outside of

[21] Cf. below, pp. 11, 13.

itself. Spirit, on the other hand, is self-contained. Matter has its substance outside of itself; Spirit, on the other hand, has its being within itself, and this, precisely, is Freedom.[22]

Freedom, like Spirit, is dynamic; it progresses dialectically against its own obstacles. It is never given; it must always be fought for. Every slackening of Spirit means falling back into the inertia of Matter, which means the destruction of Freedom: either when men are subject to Matter—as in poverty, sickness, cold, famine—or when they are subject to other men and used by them like things. On the other hand, Spirit, in thus overcoming its own obstacles and working itself out in history, is continuously creative; but its creativeness is not of anything ontologically new, it is predetermined in the pure potentiality of the pure Idea. It is the Idea itself, Reason, that works itself out in history. Spirit, in creating itself in time, creates the "second realm" of reality, after that of Nature. Thus it completes the world, which is both Nature and Spirit. The Spirit's own self-consciousness is, therefore, at the same time the world's own self-consciousness; it is world-consciousness. Since the world is completed, or self-completing existence, existence itself is self-consciousness; and in every existent, in so far as it is real, there is self-consciousness. This gives the Hegelian presentation sometimes a panpsychic tinge, as in the example of the elements fighting themselves in the building of a house.[23] The essentiality of self-consciousness for existence is part of the Hegelian dialectic. For how else could each natural thing "seek" to transcend itself dialectically? A trace of Spirit, of consciousness, must already be in the natural realm. The same goes for the concept itself in pure logic. The universal "strives" toward the particular, and the particular "strives" toward the universal. This striving is given in the very nature of God's will, which is the source of all creation. Only in the human realm does it fully emerge in self-consciousness.

[22] See below, pp. 23f.

[23] See below, pp. 34f. Also cf. p. 64, where Hegel speaks of the universal soul of all particulars.

3. THE NATIONAL SPIRIT

Once Spirit appears on the historical scene, it is not an abstraction but a fact. Spirit appears in concrete actuality both as universal and as particular; for the purely abstract principle, as Hegel never tires to tell us, is nowhere in existence. Spirit is a universal whose particulars are existent, namely, men and peoples. There must be in actuality the ever-disappearing particular which enforces and re-enforces, by its death and transfiguration, the universal. The latter in turn, though in longer temporal phases, dies and transforms itself, always more closely approaching to the pure Idea of Spirit. Thus we get the dialectic opposition of individual and people and of people and World Spirit. The World Spirit, as embodied in a people, is "the principle of the people," the National Spirit or *Volksgeist;* and the individuals, in so far as they are historically active, embody the *Volksgeist* and through it the World Spirit itself. Thus the primary "individuals," in which Spirit or Freedom embodies itself most immediately and directly, are the peoples and nations of the earth—but seen not with the eyes of narrow nationalists, but with those of the cosmic philosopher. By a state or nation Hegel understands a culture or civilization, an organization of freedom. Freedom, in the sense not of license but of organized liberty, is possible only in states. Therefore there is no history unless there are organized states. The National Spirit as a differentiation of the universal Spirit defines the whole cultural life of a people; it gives it its national *Gestalt,* its cultural climate and atmosphere.

Here Hegel has been badly misunderstood. If his "State" is understood too narrowly, stupidities ensue which do not lie in his meaning, even though at times narrow nationalism may not have been foreign to him. It is true, perhaps, as a modern writer holds, that the young Hegel wanted to become the German Machiavelli; [24] but the older, and thus real, Hegel—

[24] Sabine, *A History of Political Theory,* 1950, p. 635.

for also in Hegel himself the Spirit progressed toward its
reality—far outgrew such immature beginnings. When he
spoke of a state, he meant an ideal—that is, in his sense a
more and more real—state, and an actual state only in so far
as it contained the ideal elements. Therefore it is quite true
that a state may be Spirit become concrete and that the
spiritual nature of an individual may find its completion in
a state. In the organization of the state, Spirit achieves concrete objectivity, which supplements the subjectivity of the
individual as such. Nor is it paradoxical to say that a state
—that is, a civilization, a culture with all its institutions of law
and religion, art and philosophy—is "the divine Idea as it
exists on earth," that is, the divine Idea in relatively highest
actualization. Does not in such a culture the individual become conscious of himself as a cultural individual and only
thus have the possibility of developing his capacities, that is,
his full freedom? [25] This implies, on the other hand, that a
collective organization which keeps only the form but not the
content of what Hegel calls the "State," a bureaucratic power
without a culture, or, even worse, a pseudo-state which uses
this formal power to destroy all cultural content and all individual development within it, is a monstrosity, the very opposite of a state. Hegel did indeed think of such a "state," although he could never imagine its whole ghastliness. Of such
a state, he says, nothing but ruins must remain.[26] But such a
state is not the State in the Hegelian sense. It is what Hegel
calls "rotten existence," a dialectic negation of the state, which
must perish. It is the state of the rabble, which "would only
be a shapeless wild blind force, like that of a stormy elemental sea," only more destructive. There is no doubt that he
would have regarded the Hitlerian Third Reich as such a
negation of the very essence of the State. He would see in its
ruins today the necessary consequence of its evil, that is, anti-
ideal, anti-spiritual, merely sensuous and mechanical existence. In this sense this "state" was not historical; it did not

[25] See below, pp. 38, 49, 66.
[26] See below, p. 91.

partake of History as the self-development of Freedom, but only of the countermovement against History over which History continuously passes in developing itself. It was the very opposite of a state.[27]

The People is a concretion of Spirit or, logically speaking, an instance of it. Inasmuch as it develops its principles, it grows into its universality. When it forgets and neglects them, it falls away from it. In these principles the people finds its own consciousness of itself. At the height of its development, by the very dialectic of the process—for otherwise the development would not be at its height—it ceases to strive onward. It leans backward and, as it were, enjoys what it has achieved. Thus it turns culmination into decline. At that point reflection flourishes, arts and philosophy arise, but the will—the temporal actualization of the divine will in this form and fashion—slackens. Gradually the People dies off. In this very act, however, the national and thus particular spirit returns to its universality, enriched by the latest experience. It thus elevates itself over the actual phase reached, and prepares itself for the next phase, in another people. Thus history, through national cultures, is the process of the Spirit progressing to its own self, its own cumulative concept of itself, from nation to nation. The understanding of a civilization of its own self leads its spirit on toward other civilizations, where again the World Spirit appears in some individuals, begins to know itself, and finally shapes the new people into a new civilization full of historical significance. The totality of all such civilizations is the Idea as it has completed itself in absolute fullness in infinite time—the absolute Idea. Art, religion, philosophy, created by finite states, transcend in cosmic significance the states from which they sprang; they are the pure Spirit purely achieved. Beyond the State, as the objective Spirit, lies the absolute Idea. In this sphere the individual is at home in a higher sense than as citizen. Here he is man as creator— artist, saint, and philosopher.

[27] This thesis has been developed by Franz Neumann in *Behemoth*, New York, 1944.

4. THE FOUR KINDS OF MEN

There is, then, in man a sphere which the state cannot touch.[28] This sphere of individual as against political morality has been neglected by Hegel's interpreters, partly, probably, because he never developed it as clearly as political morality. But it is a definite and necessary part of his philosophy of history. We have, in all, four kinds of men in our text: the citizen, the person, the hero, and the victim—or, as we can also say, the sustainer, the transcender, the subject, and the object of history. The morality of the citizen is that of the state; the morality of the person is that of the absolute Idea; the morality of the hero is that of the World Spirit; and the morality of the victim is that of the private situation, which historically does not count. Let us briefly discuss these four kinds of men.

(a) THE CITIZEN

Since what is rational is real and what is real is as it ought to be, and the state is the rationally universal, the citizen as the particular of this state is always rational, real, and as he ought to be, that is, moral. His particular rationality is fulfilled in the state. Yet, this is not absolute rationality. For the state itself is only a phase in history; it is never the culmination, the final point of the progress of consciousness in freedom which is world history. The state is morality only in so far as morality is actualized on earth at the time. Again, only one particular state is such an actualization, that state, namely, whose "principle" is at the same time the embodiment of the World Spirit. There are other states which are not such embodiments, either because they have not yet reached or have already passed this stage at another time or because, due to their special circumstances, they are not fit for it. Their citizens, presumably, are less "moral" in the present sense of the word than those of the state which happens to be the repre-

[28] See below, pp. 45, 48.

sentative of the World Spirit in this phase. Though Hegel is not clear on this point, it is certain that his "State," at least in certain aspects, is not *any* state but that state which incorporates the maximum ideal at the time. It is the state whose ambitions and strivings coincide with and complete those of the citizens, where every citizen finds his own fulfillment. "A state is then well constituted and internally powerful when the private interest of its citizens is one with the common interest of the state, and one finds its gratification and realization in the other." [29] Thus Hegel fuses, through the dialectic method, the development of the individual with that of all mankind, in its culmination at the time.

Since particulars alone can make no universal, citizens alone cannot be the consciousness of freedom. Only the state as a whole, their culture, actualizes freedom. Individual freedom alone is capriciousness, arbitrariness, which must be subordinated to the universal freedom as concreted in a national culture. Indeed, the story of individuals alone, and even of individuals in the still emotional, irrational community of the family, is not yet history. History is the progress of the *consciousness* of freedom. The moment the individual is *conscious* of his freedom, he is the citizen of the moral state, the member of a cultural community. The state, not he himself, is the universal of his freedom; he himself is only an instance. This stage of development can be transcended, in the absolutely moral man, the person, and in the historically moral man, the hero. But even they must be, or have been, citizens. Thus Hegel can say that no mere persons are moral [30] and that even in the crude primitive state the individual will does not and must not count.[31] This thought, spun out, leads to the individual who is of neither moral nor historical import, the fourth man, the victim. How this fits into true morality and Hegel's scheme we shall see in a moment. But it must be clear that from his premise—that the state is the "ex-

29 See below, p. 30.
30 See below, p. 56.
31 See below, p. 50.

ternally existing, genuinely moral life . . . the unity of the universal and essential with the subjective will; and as such . . . *Morality*" [32]—it follows that "the individual who lives in this unity has a moral life, a value which consists in this substantiality alone. . . . The laws of ethics are not accidental, but are rationality itself. It is the end of the state to make the substantial prevail and maintain itself in the actual doings and convictions of men." [33] It is this view of states that inspired Walt Whitman. Totalitarians can find no comfort in it. Freedom purely subjective is capriciousness, but Freedom universalized in the concrete form of a civilization is objective, and thus concrete morality. Its objective form is law.[34] "*In summary*," Hegel tells us, "*the vitality of the state in individuals is what we call Morality.*" [35] It was the vagueness and abstractness of the individual moral law, especially the Kantian, which led Hegel to this concretion of the moral law in the law of the state. The state thus became the order of rational wills, and the rational will is free when and in so far as it is part of and follows this order.

But this Hegelian construction was historically most dangerous, partly because Hegel never made sufficiently clear what he meant by the "State," partly because his readers forgot what he did tell them. The moment "State" is understood to mean *any* state, Hegel's position becomes absurd and his citizen a caricature of morality. Then it is possible to present as Hegel's view that only the citizen is subject to the law, and hence to morality, but that the state is outside of it—whereas actually the Hegelian state, the very moment it loses sight of morality, begins its historical decline. Or Hegel is compared to Hobbes, according to whom obedience to the state is the greatest civil duty—and it is forgotten that the Hobbesian

---

[32] *Ibid.*

[33] *Ibid.*

[34] See below, pp. 53ff.

[35] See below, p. 66. Individual morality (*Moralität*) here fuses with national ethos (*Sittlichkeit*). Hegel does not always keep to his distinction of these terms.

state is not a moral state in the Hegelian sense but a pragmatic institution to guarantee law and order. It is not the meeting point of the World Spirit and the individual spirit. True enough, Hegel himself sometimes suggests such an interpretation, when the state, no matter what its moral content, is regarded as that to which blind obedience must be given, as at one or two points in our text.[36] But there is no blind duty of obedience for the Hegelian citizen; there is a coincidence of character and inclination between the rational citizen and his state. Again, his statement that the state is not here for the citizen but the citizen owes everything to the state [37] has been misconstrued in the totalitarian sense, when actually it means that the state is that creation which gives the individual the field of action for his innate rational striving.[38] His statement that that which is, is what ought to be has been misunderstood as mere opportunism. Yet it makes good moral sense when by "State" is understood the structure of rational wills. Only such a state is historically effective in the sense of contributing to the cumulative effort that is the World Spirit. Therefore it is indeed true that that which historically is, is that which ideally ought to be. On the other hand, of course, it must be said that Hegel's careless way of expression and the influence of his feudal German environment open the way to these and other misunderstandings. By no stretch of the imagination can Hegel be called a democrat in the sense of his French or American contemporaries. He has little conception of the dignity and importance of the citizen as such, and in our text he caricatures the most vital political functions of democracy, such as voting, which for him is nothing but an arithmetical counting which the democratic statesman has to read off as the weatherman does the barometer, and act accordingly.[39]

[36] E.g., p. 53, where the Athenian's instinctive obedience is praised against the reflective obedience of the modern.

[37] See below, p. 52.

[38] This morality is similar to that described by Bradley in "My Station and Its Duty," *Ethical Studies,* Library of Liberal Arts. Cf. below, p. 37.

[39] See below, p. 57.

He does not see, as did Kant, the incompatibility of military and democratic organization, and therefore uses the military as his only example for the necessity of obedience in democracy.[40] That he thus defeats his own definition of the state and of the citizen's morality in it he does not seem to see. The military organization is not one of rational wills. In war democracy is suspended. For Hegel, on the other hand, war is one of the cultural expressions of the state; [41] or rather, as the means for the destruction of states, it is for him the negative to the creation of states. Whereas the latter is a moral act by which the rationality of the Idea is fulfilled, the former is the act by which the immoral, the irrational, is destroyed. But Hegel does not examine the question whether the victor is always the moral.

(b) THE PERSON

The morality of the citizen is only relative morality. There is a deeper recess of the human spirit which is beyond the state, and which is the abode of absolute morality. The state is, as we have seen, only *relatively* the highest development of the rational. The universal as the potentially absolute resides within the human heart and mind; and this absolute is not touched by the state, except when the state is the Absolute itself, which it will be only at the end of history—if there ever is one. Man as the absolutely moral being, the Human Person—rather than as the relatively moral being, the Citizen—makes a fleeting appearance on our pages. His morality is intrinsic and personal, as against the extrinsic and social morality of the citizen. There is an element in man "which is absolutely not subordinate," not even to the cunning of Reason; indeed, not even to the course of history itself, but which "exists in individuals as inherently eternal and divine." [42]

40 *Ibid.*

41 But it is false to say that he glorified war. See H. G. ten Bruggencate, "Hegel's Views on War," *The Philosophical Quarterly*, Vol. I, No. 1, October, 1950.

42 See below, pp. 44, 48.

This "morality, ethics, and religion" is neither given, guaranteed, nor supplemented by the state. It exists absolutely. Man, in this sense, is an end in himself; he possesses divinity. And his divinity is not subject to development, but exists in its absolute form. This is his absolute Freedom, by and through which man is self-responsible. No matter how circumscribed the circumstances of his life, this inward morality has infinite, absolute value. "It is quite shut out from the noisy din of world history," both from its contingent and its necessary, dialectically logical implications.[43]

Here, then, is a realm which falls outside of world history and even, it seems, of the whole Hegelian scheme, at least as far as Hegel has developed it. But for this matter, this inner human being is not exempt from dialectic, not even from Hegelian dialectic. Rather, we have here another strand of Hegelian influence, which leads through Kierkegaard to the Existentialists. In our text Hegel never makes completely clear the difference in the two meanings of morality, the relative and the absolute, probably because he himself was not entirely clear about it. For this reason some of his interpreters are right when they say that he misunderstands the problem of the individual.[44] But others are equally right when they maintain that he is the one philosopher who gives a systematic place to the unique value of the individual, and thus stands in opposition to the whole course of Western philosophy from Plato to Kant, which treated systematically only the universal and abstract, never the uniquely concrete.[45]

(c) THE HERO

Between the man of relative or social morality and the man of absolute or personal morality stands the historic hero, in whom the uniquely individual fuses with the universally so-

[43] See below, p. 48.

[44] Cf. Sabine, *op. cit.*, p. 653. Kierkegaard himself was of this opinion and therefore developed his existential dialectic in opposition to Hegel.

[45] August Messer, *Geschichte der Philosophie von Kant bis Hegel*, Leipzig, 1932, p. 119.

cial—with the World Spirit in its course toward the absolute
Idea from one historically relative phase to the next. This is
a third kind of man in our text. In him the historical situation concentrates itself. As an individual, with all his drives
and powers, he is nothing but the raw material of the World
Spirit, which grasps him with an all-consuming historic passion. Thus the abstract Spirit acquires concrete power of
actualization. The individual as raw material for the historical
efficacy of the World Spirit is primarily power, the motor force
of history, whose direction is prescribed by the Spirit. Hegel
puts the emphasis on the direction; other writers, such as
Goethe, have put it on the power. But even Hegel, much like
Goethe, speaks of the almost animalic identity of the passion
of man with the idea of Spirit.[46]

In such historic men the capriciousness of inclinations and
desires is not merged in the objective law of the state, as in
the citizen, but rather in the demands of the World Spirit
itself, which, with their help, produces these laws. They are,
so to speak, the still fluid form of the future state and its
institutions. Their morality is not that of the state but that
of creating the state. It is the creative idea of the future state
itself. The World Spirit knocks, as Hegel says, through them
at the surface of actuality, ready to break what is, like a
shell. The source of the hero's power is still hidden under
the surface of actuality; he has direct access to the reality of
the Idea, and it inspires him to his deeds, filling his whole
being with concentrated will and thus making him the subject of history, the creator of it, who brings to birth what is
still hidden in the womb of time. It is the heroic man who
pushes history forward. On the other hand, the Hegelian hero
is completely guided by the World Spirit, and the World
Spirit uses him, cunningly, for its own ends. The hero does
not influence the World Spirit. There is no ontological spon-
taneity in him that infuses into the Idea what was not in it
before he appeared.

[46] See below, p. 42. Cf. Goethe, *Dichtung und Wahrheit*, Pt. IV, Bk. 20
(on the "Daemonic").

This strict predetermination even in detail is not a necessity of the Hegelian system. On the contrary, it contradicts it. The particular, in the system, is an equal partner in the dialectic game. The universal does not "use" it; it gets its full nature in and through it. So does the World Spirit in and through the hero. The hero could contribute more than mere existence to the Spirit. His morality is not derived merely from the Spirit, but also from the personal sources of what we called our second kind of man. If Hegel had developed this kind of man more, he could have inserted spontaneous individuality into the course of history. But he did not do it. The course of history is impersonal. From this it follows that the historic hero himself becomes impersonal and rides roughshod over "less historical" individuals. Hegel is pained by this, but there is the overriding necessity of the logical development of the Idea. Here, then, appears a lack in Hegel's moral foundations. His third man gains over the second, with the result that the fourth man appears, the victim. Morality is more a collective than an individual matter for Hegel; and the great man becomes, if "necessary," an immoral force. Here the modern totalitarians can and do take their departure; libertarians like Mill get nauseated, and Hegel, in so far as he becomes a historic hero himself, for the prophets of Left and Right totalitarianism, becomes the father of immoral deeds.

(d) THE VICTIM

The historic hero, through his insight and energy, is the subject of history. The human individual without such insight and energy is the object of history, its victim. He is, in a way, guilty of his own death and suffering because he does not rise to the occasion, the human possibilities of seeing the wholeness of the historical situation. His morality is a fourth kind of morality, beside that of the citizen, whose morality is the State; that of the ethical person, whose morality is the absolute Idea; and that of the hero, whose morality is the Spirit. This fourth morality is that of the circumscribed private situation. The victim is the private man or woman who prefers happiness to greatness. Hegel does not see the greatness of happiness, the art of the individual in shaping his life and successfully linking the succession of life situations. Such ethics of private success is not for Hegel. The private individual shuts himself up in small circumstances and thus isolates himself from the World Spirit and its process. History marches on over him. In this sense "the history of the world moves on a higher level than that of morality" [47]—again a thought which has been widely misunderstood, simply because this kind of morality has been confused with the other kinds. An individual may be perfectly moral in this sense and obstruct the course of history, or he may be immoral in this sense and advance it.[48] To be historically effective and, in some cases, even to survive, it is not sufficient to be morally good in the private sense. One must be wide-awake to the historical situation and thus rise to the higher morality of the Spirit. Many in the private sense "good" men and women in our time, as in past ages, have lost their lives because of historical shortsightedness and kept it because of historical awareness.

But no matter whether the individual does or does not see the historical situation, he is part of it. In this respect his fate is historical fate; he is historical material. The cunning of Reason uses both, the wide-awake and the sleepy, for its ends—the ones for a grand historical role, of which violent but historically significant death may be a part; the others for the smaller role of the individual of the mass who may die in the same way, though seemingly senselessly. Thus man as a particular is always outwitted and deceived by the World Spirit, whether he is its agent or its victim; only that the victim appears also as the victim of the agent. That the agent, the hero, is also the victim of the victims is seldom observed. But Hegel makes it clear. He shows how the hero is decried, envied, and betrayed; his work misunderstood and forced into the smallness of the small minds of historical

[47] See below, p. 82.
[48] Ibid.

lackeys and parasites.[49] Thus, although our text sometimes reads bloodthirstily—"the mighty form of the hero must trample down many an innocent flower"—it is not Hegel who must be condemned but history. The weak ones are those who cannot read the signs of the times. What happens to them is the same as happens to the pedestrian who disregards the traffic signals. Rather than bewail this fact, we should open our eyes to history and help others to do so. If we see the juggernaut of history advance, in its dialectically negative phase, we do not necessarily have to join or be crushed. We can get out of its way, as did most of the European emigrants to America. If we don't, our only other alternative is the doubly tragic role of Cassandra, of vainly warning the blind and falling with them. Then we are not true victims; we choose our fall more clear-sightedly than the hero chooses his rise. For we know we will fall, but he does not. The true victim of history is the blind. Thus the tragedy of history is largely one of human stupidity.

The historical material of Spirit, man, is still imperfect. It is, precisely, the purpose of history to perfect man more and more. This, for Hegel, is history's overriding aim. He sees history purely teleologically and excludes all the contingent, tracing the grand outline only of the cosmic drama whose human detail is often tragedy. In seeing history this way, he remains, in spite of his efforts at being concrete, often quite abstract. Especially, in seeing the victim of history as simply punished for his lack of insight, he abstracts from the fullness of man, who is not only a private person and as such failing to live up to history, but also a moral person with a right to secede from it. It is this person, our second man, who falls victim to history together with the fourth. That is, the wholeness of man falls victim to the failure of one of his aspects. This neglect of the intrinsic morality of man within the univeral progress of Reason is the principal shortcoming of Hegel's philosophy of history. Its emphasis on freedom thus lacks a most obvious foundation. The humanity of man, the center of

[49] See below, pp. 42f.

Hebrew-Christian religion, is seen in the organizational freedom of a state rather than in the privacy of man's conscience. What Hegel, mainly through Marx, has historically wrought is an antithesis against the Middle Ages: social efficiency against Christian morality. The task of our time seems to be to bring about a synthesis of the two.

NOTE ON TEXT

The German text of Hegel's "Lectures on the Philosophy of History" was published posthumously. Since Hegel did not leave a final manuscript, but only lecture notes, the German edition must be considered an "edited" version, primarily, of course, based on Hegel's own notes. These notes were supplemented and clarified by students' notes, of which, fortunately, two extensive sets were found and utilized by the first editor of his work, Eduard Gans.

Gans' edition appeared in 1837. A revised and enlarged edition, edited by Hegel's son, Karl, was published in 1840. Georg Lasson edited a third and still more comprehensive edition, which was published in 1917. This last edition differs in arrangement, as well as in scope, from both the first and second.

The second edition is generally considered the most authoritative version and is followed here with a few exceptions. Interpolations from the first edition are marked in the text by footnotes; those from the third, by brackets and italics. Additions by the translator, felt necessary for greater clarity of meaning, have been put in parentheses. All footnotes are the translator's, except those designated *"Author."* Following the example of Lasson, subheadings have been inserted in order to break up the text into logical divisions of convenient length. These, however, differ from those employed by Lasson.

The following is a list of the passages of the third edition (Hegel's *Sämtliche Werke*, Leipzig, 1920, Band VIII) inserted in the text of the second edition:

Our text page	Lasson's page
17f.	20f.
20ff.	27ff.
31	65
32ff.	69ff.
33f.	70, 71
34f.	71, 61
35	62
37ff.	72, 73ff.
39	75
41f.	76, 78, 79ff.
43	83, 83
44	84
45	85
50f.	92
51f.	92ff.
52	91
93	161f.
95	165

Lasson's edition, published by Felix Meiner ("Philoso-phische Bibliothek," vol. 171a), contains on pp. 288-297 a resume of the textual history of the various German editions, which is recommended to the interested reader.

REASON IN HISTORY

A GENERAL INTRODUCTION TO
THE PHILOSOPHY OF HISTORY

1. THE THREE METHODS OF WRITING HISTORY

The subject of these lectures is the philosophy of world history. This means that we are not concerned with general deductions drawn from history, illustrated by particular examples from it, but with the nature of history itself. What we mean by history will become clear if we begin by discussing the other methods of dealing with it. There are, in all, three methods of treating history:

1. Original History
2. Reflective History
3. Philosophical History.

1. We shall get an immediate and definite picture of the first kind by mentioning a few names. Take, for example, the histories of Herodotus, Thucydides, and similar historians. They primarily described the actions, events, and conditions which they had before their own eyes and whose spirit they shared. They transferred what was externally present into the realm of mental representation and thus translated the external appearances into inner conception—much as does the poet, who transforms perceptual material into mental images. These original historians, of course, drew also upon statements and reports of others—it is impossible that one man can see everything. But the poet, too, draws on the product of others; his most priceless possession is language. The historian binds together the fleeting rush of events and deposits it for immortality in the temple of Mnemosyne. Myths, folk songs, traditions are not part of original history; they are still obscure modes and peculiar to obscure peoples. Here we deal with peoples who knew who they were and what they wanted. Observed and observable reality is a more solid foundation for history than the transience of myths and epics. Once a people

3

has reached firm individuality, such forms cease to be its historical essence.

Original historians, then, transform the events, actions, and
situations present to them into a work of representative
thought. Hence, the content of such history cannot be of large
external scope—consider, for example, Herodotus, Thucydides,
Guicciardini;[1] their essential subject is what is actual and living in their environment. The culture of the author and that
of the events created in his work, the spirit of the author and
that of the actions he relates are one and the same. He describes what he has, more or less, experienced, or at least wit-
nessed as a contemporary. He deals with short periods of time,
individual presentations of men and events. Out of individual,
unreflected features he composes his portrait in order to bring
it before posterity as distinctly as he experienced it in person
or in the personal accounts of others. He is not concerned
with reflections *about* the events. He lives the spirit of the
events; he does not yet transcend them. If, like Caesar, he
belongs to the rank of the military or political leaders, then
it is his very own aims which appear as history.

When we say here that such an historian does not reflect
about events, but that persons and peoples appear themselves
in his work, we seem to be contradicted by the orations which
can be read, for example, in Thucydides. It is certainly true
that they have never been made in this form. But speeches
are actions among men and, indeed, most effective ones. True
enough, people often say they were *merely* talks and thus supposedly insignificant. But *such* talk is merely chatter, and
chatter has the important advantage of being historically insignificant. But speeches from peoples to peoples or to peoples
and princes are integral parts of history. Even granted, therefore, that orations like those of Pericles—that most profoundly
accomplished, most genuine, and most noble of statesmen—
had been elaborated by Thucydides, they were yet not foreign
to Pericles' character. In these orations these men expressed

[1] Francesco Guicciardini (1483-1540), in his *Istoria d'Italia* (published
1561-64), treats the period from 1492 to 1534.

the maxims of their people, of their own personality, the consciousness of their political situation, and the principles of their moral and spiritual nature, their aims and actions. What the historian puts into their mouths is not a borrowed consciousness but the speaker's own mind.

There are not as many historians as one may think whose close and continued study is necessary if we want to re-live the life of nations and enter into their spirit—historians who give us not only scholarship but deep and genuine enjoyment. We have already mentioned Herodotus, the father and founder of history, and Thucydides; Xenophon's *Anabasis* is an equally original work; Caesar's *Commentaries* are the simple masterpiece of a great mind. In antiquity these historians were necessarily great captains and rulers. In the Middle Ages, if we except the bishops who stood in the center of political events, the monks, as naïve writers of chronicles, were as much isolated from, as the men of antiquity were connected with, the course of events. In modern times all this has changed. Our minds are primarily conceptual and immediately transform all events into reports for communication. We have excellent works of this type—simple and concise ones—mainly about military events, which can well be compared with those of Caesar and even exceed them in wealth of information and description of techniques and circumstances. Here also belong the French "Memoirs." They are often written by witty men about small areas of events and with an abundance of anecdotes, so that their historical basis is rather thin; but some, as those of Cardinal von Retz,[2] are true historical masterpieces, which survey a larger historical field. Germany has few such masters: Frederick the Great with his *Histoire de Mon Temps* is a noteworthy exception. Such men must really be of high social position. Only when one stands on high ground can one survey the situation and note every detail, not when one has to peer up from below through a small hole.

2. The second method of history may be called the *reflec-*

---

[2] Jean François Paul de Condi, Cardinal von Retz (1614-79), Archbishop of Paris and leader of the Fronde.

tive. It is that kind of history which transcends the present—not in time but in spirit. Here we must distinguish several kinds:

(a) The first is *universal* history, that is, the survey of the entire history of a people, a country, or the world. Here the main thing is the elaboration of the historical material. The historian achieves this with his own spirit, which is different from the spirit of the material. What is important here is, on the one hand, the principle with which the author approaches the content and meaning of the actions and events he describes, and, on the other hand, his own method of writing history. With us Germans, reflection and understanding vary greatly in these respects; each historian insists on his own peculiar ways and manners. The English and French have a more general knowledge of how to write history. They are on a higher level of universal and national culture. With us everybody invents something peculiar for himself, and instead of writing history we keep on trying to find out how history ought to be written.

This first kind of reflective history connects with original history if it has no other purpose than to present the totality of a country's history. Such compilations—as those of Livy, of Diodorus of Sicily, and Müller's "History of Switzerland" [3]—are most commendable when well done. In this case it is best, of course, for the writer to approximate closely the first mode and write so plastically that the reader gets the impression that he is listening to contemporaries and eyewitnesses of the events. But the individuality of spirit which must characterize a writer who belongs to a certain cultural period is frequently not in accord with the spirit that runs through the period he writes about. The spirit that speaks out of the writer is quite different from that of the times he describes. Thus Livy makes his old Roman kings, consuls, and generals speak in the fashion of accomplished lawyers of the Livian era, which contrasts strikingly with the genuine traditions of Roman antiquity,

---

[3] Johannes von Müller (1752-1809), *Schweizergeschichten*, 24 vols., written 1780-1808, published 1810.

such as the fable of Menenius Agrippa.[4] Livy also gives us descriptions of battles as if he had seen them himself; but their features are simply features of battles of any period. And their distinctness contrasts further with the lack of connection and the inconsistency in his treatment of other, often essential, features. The difference between such a compiler and an original historian may best be seen when one compares the work of Livy with that of Polybius, and the manner in which Livy uses, expands, and abridges the historical periods which are preserved in Polybius' account. Johannes von Müller, in order to be true to the times he describes, has given his history a stilted, hollowly solemn, pedantic character. One does better to read these things in old Tschudi,[5] where everything is more naïve and natural without such artificial, affected archaism.

A history of this kind, which endeavors to survey long periods or the whole of world history, must give up the individual presentation of reality and abridge itself by means of abstractions, not only in the sense of leaving out events and actions, but also in the sense of making thought itself the mightiest epitomist. A battle, a great victory, a siege are no longer themselves; they are concentrated in simple statements. When Livy speaks of the wars with the Volsci he says at times shortly enough: "This year war was carried on with the Volsci."

(b) A second kind of reflective history is the *pragmatic*. In dealing with the past and occupying ourselves with a remote world, there opens up for the mind an actuality which arises out of its own activity and as reward for its labor. The events are many, but their universal idea and their inner connection are one. This nullifies the past and makes the event present. Pragmatic reflections, no matter how abstract, belong indeed to the present, and the stories of the past are quickened into present-day life. Whether such reflections are really interesting

[4] The moral of which is that it is unwise to starve oneself to spite one's stomach.

[5] Aegidius von Tschudi (1505-72), *Schweizerchronik*, published 1734-36.

and full of life depends on the spirit of the writer. Here belong, in particular, moral reflections and the moral enlightenment to be derived from history, for the sake of which history has often been written. Although it must be said that examples of good deeds elevate the soul and should be used in the moral instruction of children in order to impress upon them moral virtue, the destiny of peoples and nations—their interests, conditions, and complicated affairs—are a different matter. One often advises rulers, statesmen, and peoples to learn from the experiences of history. But what experience and history teach is that peoples and governments have never yet learned from history, let alone acted according to its lessons. Every age has conditions of its own and is an individual situation; decisions must and can be made only within, and in accordance with, the age itself. In the turmoil of world affairs no universal principle, no memory of similar conditions in the past can help us—a vague memory has no power against the vitality and freedom of the present. Nothing is more shallow in this respect than the oft-repeated appeal to Greek and Roman examples during the French Revolution; nothing is more different than the nature of these peoples and that of our own times. Johannes von Müller had such moral intentions in his universal as well as in his Swiss history; for the enlightenment of princes, governments, and peoples, particularly the Swiss people, he prepared his own collection of lessons and reflections and often gives in his correspondence the exact number of reflections produced during the week. But he must not count these works among his best. Only the thorough, free, and comprehensive insight into situations and the deep understanding of their idea—as for example in Montesquieu's *Spirit of the Laws*—can make such reflections true and interesting. One reflective history, therefore, supersedes another. Each writer has access to the materials; each can think himself able to arrange and elaborate them and inject his spirit into them as the spirit of the ages. Weary of such reflective histories, one has frequently taken recourse to presenting events from all possible angles. Such histories are, it is true, of some value, but they offer mostly raw material. We Germans are content with them; the French, however, spiritedly create a present for themselves and refer the past to the present state of affairs.

(c) The third kind of reflective history is the *critical*. It must be mentioned, for this is the mode in which in present-day Germany history is written. It is not history itself which is presented here, but rather history of historiography: evaluation of historical narratives and examination of their truth and trustworthiness. The outstanding feature of this method, in point of fact and of intention, consists in the acuteness of the author who wrests results from narrations rather than from events.[6] The French have here given us much that is profound and judicious. But they have not attempted to pass off such a purely critical procedure as historical; rather, they have presented their evaluations in the form of critical treatises. With us, the so-called "higher criticism" has taken possession not only of all philology but also of historical literature. This higher criticism has then served to justify the introduction of all kinds of unhistorical monstrosities of pure imagination. Here we have another method of gaining actuality from history: replacing historical data by subjective fancies—fancies which are held to be the more excellent, the bolder they are, that is, the smaller their factual basis and the larger their contradiction with the most definite facts of history.

(d) The last kind of reflective history is that which presents itself openly as *fragmentary*. It is abstractive but, in adopting universal points of view—for example the history of art, of law, of religion—it forms a transition to philosophical world history. In our time this kind of conceptual history has been particularly developed and emphasized. Such branches of history refer to the whole of a people's history; the question is only whether this total context is made evident or merely shown in external relations. In the latter case they appear as purely accidental peculiarities of a people. But if such reflec-

---

[6] The text here is ambiguous. It may also be read as meaning that the outstanding feature of this method lies in the author and not in the events.

tive history succeeds in presenting general points of view and if these points of view are true, it must be conceded that such histories are more than the merely external thread and order of events and actions, that they are indeed their internal, guiding soul. For, like Mercury, the guide of souls, the Idea is in truth the guide of peoples and the world; and the Spirit, its rational and necessary will, guides and always has guided the course of world events. To learn to know it in its office of guidance is our purpose. This brings us to:

3. The third method of history, the *philosophical.* There was little in the two preceding methods that had to be clarified; their concept was self-explanatory. But it is different with this last one, which indeed seems to require some commentary or justification. The most universal definition would be that philosophy of history is nothing but the thoughtful contemplation of history. To think is one of those things we cannot help doing; in this we differ from the animals. In our sensation, cognition, and intellection, in our instincts and volitions, in as far as they are human, there is an element of thinking. But reference to thinking may here appear inadequate. In history, thinking is subordinate to the data of reality, which latter serve as guide and basis for historians. Philosophy, on the other hand, allegedly produces its own ideas out of speculation, without regard to given data. If philosophy approached history with such ideas, it may be held, it would treat history as its raw material and not leave it as it is, but shape it in accordance with these ideas, and hence construct it, so to speak, a priori. But since history is supposed to understand events and actions merely for what they are and have been, and is the truer, the more factual it is, it seems that the method of philosophy would be in contradiction to the function of history. This contradiction and the charge consequently brought against philosophy shall here be explained and refuted. But we shall not, for that matter, attempt to correct the innumerable specific misrepresentations which are current and continuously recur about the aims, interests, and methods of history, and its relations to philosophy.

II. REASON AS THE BASIS OF HISTORY

The sole thought which philosophy brings to the treatment of history is the simple concept of *Reason:* that Reason is the law of the world and that, therefore, in world history, things have come about rationally. This conviction and insight is a presupposition of history as such; in philosophy itself it is not presupposed. Through its speculative reflection philosophy has demonstrated that Reason—and this term may be accepted here without closer examination of its relation to God—is both *substance and infinite power,* in itself the infinite material of all natural and spiritual life as well as the *infinite form,* the actualization of itself as content. It is *substance,* that is to say, that by which and in which all reality has its being and subsistence. It is infinite *power,* for Reason is not so impotent as to bring about only the ideal, the ought, and to remain in an existence outside of reality—who knows where—as something peculiar in the heads of a few people. It is the infinite *content* of all essence and truth, for it does not require, as does finite activity, the condition of external materials, of given data from which to draw nourishment and objects of its activity; it supplies its own nourishment and is its own reference. And it is infinite *form,* for only in its image and by its fiat do phenomena arise and begin to live.[1] It is its own exclusive presupposition and absolutely final purpose, and itself works out this purpose from potentiality into actuality, from inward source to outward appearance, not only in the natural but also in the spiritual universe, in world history. That this *Idea* or *Reason* is the True, the Eternal, the Absolute Power and that it and nothing but it, its glory and majesty, manifests itself in the world—this, as we said before, has been proved in philosophy and is being presupposed here as proved.

Those among you, gentlemen, who are not yet acquainted

[1] This sentence, deleted in the second edition, is here restored from the first edition.

11

with philosophy could perhaps be asked to come to these lectures on world history with the belief in Reason, with a desire, a thirst for its insight. It is indeed this desire for rational insight, for cognition, and not merely for a collection of various facts, which ought to be presupposed as a subjective aspiration in the study of the sciences. For even though one were not approaching world history with the thought and knowledge of Reason, at least one ought to have the firm and invincible faith that there is Reason in history and to believe that the world of intelligence and of self-conscious willing is not abandoned to mere chance, but must manifest itself in the light of the rational Idea. Actually, however, I do not have to demand such belief in advance. What I have said here provisionally, and shall have to say later on, must, even in our branch of science, be taken as a summary view of the whole. It is not a presupposition of study; it is a *result* which happens to be known to myself because I already know the whole. Therefore, only the study of world history itself can show that it has proceeded rationally, that it represents the rationally necessary course of the World Spirit, the Spirit whose nature is indeed always one and the same, but whose one nature unfolds in the course of the world. This, as I said, must be the result of history. History itself must be taken as it is; we have to proceed historically, empirically. Among other things, we must not let ourselves be tempted by the professional historians, for these, particularly the Germans, who possess great authority, practice precisely what they accuse the philosophers of, namely, a priori historical fiction. For example, it is a widespread fabrication that there was an original, primeval people taught immediately by God, endowed with perfect insight and wisdom, possessing a thorough knowledge of all natural laws and spiritual truths; or that there were such or such sacerdotal peoples; or, to mention a more specific matter, that there was a Roman epos from which the Roman historians derived the earliest history—and so on. Apriorities [2]

---

[2] "Authorities" (*Autoritäten*) in earlier editions was a misreading. The original text is *Aprioritäten*.

of this kind we shall leave to these talented professional historians, among whom, at least in our country, their use is quite common. As our first condition we must therefore state that we apprehend the historical faithfully. In such general terms, however, as "faithfully" and "apprehend" lies an ambiguity. Even the average and mediocre historian, who perhaps believes and pretends that he is merely receptive, merely surrendering himself to the data, is not passive in his thinking. He brings his categories with him and sees the data through them. In everything that is supposed to be scientific, Reason must be awake and reflection applied. To him who looks at the world rationally the world looks rationally back. The relation is mutual. But we cannot treat here the various modes of reflection, of points of view, of judgment, not even those concerning the relative importance or unimportance of facts—the most elementary category.

Only two aspects of the general conviction that Reason has ruled in the world and in world history may be called to your attention. They will give us an immediate opportunity to examine our most difficult question and to point ahead to the main theme.

1. The first is the historical fact of the Greek, Anaxagoras, who was the first to point out that *nous,* understanding in general or Reason, rules the world—but not an intelligence in the sense of an individual consciousness, not a spirit as such. These two must be carefully distinguished. The motion of the solar system proceeds according to immutable laws; these laws are its reason. But neither the sun nor the planets, which according to these laws rotate around it, have any consciousness of it. Thus, the thought that there is Reason in nature, that nature is ruled by universal, unchangeable laws, does not surprise us; we are used to it and make very little of it. Also, this historical circumstance teaches us a lesson of history: things which may seem trivial to us have not always been in the world; a new thought like this one marks an epoch in the development of the human spirit. Aristotle says of Anaxagoras, as the originator of this thought, that he ap-

peared like a sober man among the drunken. From Anaxagoras, Socrates adopted the doctrine, which became forthwith
the ruling idea in philosophy, except in the school of Epicu-
rus, who ascribed all events to chance. "I was delighted about
this," Plato makes Socrates say, "and hoped to have found a
teacher who would interpret Nature by Reason and would
show me in the particular its particular purpose, and in the
universal, the universal purpose. I should not have given up
this hope for anything. But how greatly was I disappointed
when, having zealously applied myself to the writings of
Anaxagoras, I found that he mentions only external causes,
such as Air, Ether, Water, and the like, instead of Reason." [3]
It is evident that the insufficiency which Socrates found in the
principle of Anaxagoras has nothing to do with the principle
itself, but with Anaxagoras' failure to apply it to concrete
nature. Nature was not understood or comprehended through
this principle; the principle remained abstract—nature was
not understood as a development of Reason, as an organization brought forth by it. I wish at the very outset to draw your
attention to this difference between a concept, a principle, a
truth, as confined to the abstract and as determining concrete
application and development. This difference is fundamental;
among other things we shall come back to precisely this point
at the end of our world history, when we deal with the most
recent political events.

2. The second point is the historical connection of the
thought that Reason rules the world with another form of it,
well known to us—that of religious truth: that the world is
not abandoned to chance and external accident but controlled
by *Providence*. I said before that I do not make any demand
on your belief in the principle announced; but I think I may
appeal to this belief in its religious form, unless the nature
of scientific philosophy precludes, as a general rule, the acceptance of any presuppositions; or, seen from another angle,

[3] *Phaedo*, 97-98. Hegel paraphrases this passage. Cf. Plato's *Phaedo*,
translated by F. J. Church, edited by F. H. Anderson (New York, Liberal
Arts Press), pp. 50f.

unless the science itself which we want to develop should first give the proof, if not of the truth, at least of the correctness of our principle. The truth that a Providence, that is to say, a divine Providence, presides over the events of the world corresponds to our principle; for divine Providence is wisdom endowed with infinite power which realizes its own aim, that is, the absolute, rational, final purpose of the world. Reason is Thought determining itself in absolute freedom.

On the other hand, a difference, indeed an opposition, now appears between this faith and our principle, very much like that between Socrates' expectation and the principle of Anaxagoras. For this faith is also indefinite, it is what is called faith in Providence in general; it is not followed up in definite application to the whole, the comprehensive course of world history. To explain history means to reveal the passions of men, their genius, their active powers. This definiteness of Providence is usually called its *plan*. Yet this very plan is supposed to be hidden from our view; indeed, the wish to recognize it is deemed presumption. The ignorance of Anaxagoras about the manifestation of Reason in reality was naïve; the knowledge of the principle had not yet developed, either in him or in Greece in general. He was not yet able to apply his general principle to the concrete, to deduce the latter from the former. Only Socrates took the first step in comprehending the union of the concrete and the universal. Anaxagoras, then, was not opposed to such application; but the faith in Providence *is*. It is opposed at least to the application at large of our principle, to the *cognition* of the plan of Providence. In particular cases, it is true, one allows it here and there, when pious minds see in particular events not only chance but God's will—when, for example, an individual in great perplexity and need gets unexpected help. But these instances are limited to the particular purposes of this individual. In world history the "individuals" that we have to deal with are peoples; they are totalities which are states. We cannot, therefore, be satisfied with what we may call this "retail" view of faith in Providence, nor with the merely abstract, undeter-

mined faith in the universal statement that there is a
Providence, without determining its definite acts. On the contrary, we must seriously try to recognize the ways of Providence, its means and manifestations in history, and their relation to our universal principle.

But in mentioning at all the recognition of the plan of
divine Providence I have touched on a prominent question
of the day, the question, namely, whether it is possible to
recognize God—or, since it has ceased to be a question, the
doctrine, which has now become a prejudice, that it is impossible to know God. Following this doctrine we now contradict
what the Holy Scripture commands as our highest duty,
namely, not only to love but also to know God. We now cate-
gorically deny what is written, namely, that it is the spirit
which leads to truth, knows all things, and penetrates even
the depths of divinity. Thus, in placing the Divine Being
beyond our cognition and the pale of all human things, we
gain the convenient license of indulging in our own fancies.
We are freed from the necessity of referring our knowledge
to the True and Divine. On the contrary, the vanity of knowledge and the subjectivity of sentiment now have ample justification. And pious humility, in keeping true recognition of
God at arm's length, knows very well what it gains for its
arbitrary and vain striving.

I wanted to discuss the connection of our thesis—that Reason governs and has governed the world—with the question
of the possible knowledge of God, chiefly in order to mention
the accusation that philosophy avoids, or must avoid, the discussion of religious truths because it has, so to speak, a bad
conscience about them. On the contrary, the fact is that in
recent times philosophy has had to take over the defense of
religious truths against many a theological system. In the
Christian religion God has revealed Himself, which means He
has given man to understand what He is, and thus is no
longer concealed and secret. With this *possibility* of knowing
God the *obligation* to know Him is imposed upon us. God
wishes no narrow souls and empty heads for his children; He

wishes our spirit, of itself indeed poor, rich in the knowledge of Him and holding this knowledge to be of supreme value. The development of the thinking spirit only *began* with this revelation of divine essence. It must now advance to the intellectual comprehension of that which originally was present only to the feeling and imagining spirit.

[*Feeling is the lowest form in which any mental content can exist. God is the Eternal Being in and for itself; and what is universal in and for itself is subject of thought, not of feeling. It is true that everything spiritual, every content of consciousness, anything that is product and subject of thought—in particular religion and morality—must also, and originally does, exist in the mode of feeling. But feeling is not the fount from which this content flows to man, but only a primal mode in which it exists in him. It is indeed the worst mode, a mode which he has in common with the animal. What is substantial must also exist in feeling, but it does mainly exist in a higher, more dignified form. If one wants to relegate the moral, the true, the most spiritual mental content necessarily to feeling and emotion and keep it there on general principle, one would ascribe to it essentially the animalic form; but this is not at all capable of containing the spirit. In feeling, the mental content is the smallest possible; it is present in its lowest possible form. As long as it is still in feeling it is veiled and entirely indefinite. It is still entirely subjective, present exclusively in the subjective form. If one says: "I feel such and such and so and so," then one has secluded himself in himself. Everybody else has the same right to say: "I don't feel it that way." And hence one has retreated from the common soil of understanding. In wholly particular affairs feeling is entirely in its right. But to maintain that all men had this or that in their feeling is a contradiction in terms; it contradicts the concept of feeling, the point of view of the individual subjectivity of each which one has taken with this statement. As soon as mental content is placed into feeling, everybody is reduced to his subjective point of view. If someone called anyone else by this or that epithet, the other would be entitled to give it* back; and both, from their respective points of view, would be entitled to offend each other. If someone says he has religion in his feeling and the other that he does not find any God in his feeling, then both are right. If in this manner the divine content—the revelation of God, the relationship of man to God, the being of God for man—is reduced to pure feeling, then it is reduced to pure subjectivity, to the arbitrary, to whim. In this way one actually gets rid of truth as it is in and for itself. The true is universal in and for itself, essential, substantial; as such it can be only in and for thought.] The time has finally come to understand also the rich product of creative Reason which is world history.

It was for a while the fashion to admire God's wisdom in animals, plants, and individual lives. If it is conceded that Providence manifests itself in such objects and materials, why not also in world history? Because its scope seems to be too large. But the divine wisdom, or Reason, is the same in the large as in the small. We must not deem God too weak to exercise his wisdom on a grand scale. Our intellectual striving aims at recognizing that what eternal wisdom *intended* it has actually *accomplished,* dynamically active in the world, both in the realm of nature and that of the spirit. In this respect our method is a theodicy, a justification of God, which Leibniz attempted metaphysically, in his way, by undetermined abstract categories. Thus the evil in the world was to be comprehended and the thinking mind reconciled with it. Nowhere, actually, exists a larger challenge to such reconciliation than in world history. This reconciliation can only be attained through the recognition of the positive elements in which that negative element disappears as something subordinate and vanquished. This is possible through the consciousness, on the one hand, of the true ultimate purpose of the world and, on the other hand, of the fact that this purpose has been actualized in the world and that the evil cannot ultimately prevail beside it. But for this end the mere belief in *nous* and providence is not sufficient. "Reason," which is said to govern the world, is as indefinite a term as "Providence." One always speaks of Reason without being able to indicate its definition, its content, which alone would enable us to judge whether something is rational or irrational. What we need is an adequate definition of Reason. Without such definition we can get no further than mere words. With this let us proceed to the second point that we want to consider in this introduction.

III. THE IDEA OF HISTORY AND ITS REALIZATION

The question of how Reason is determined in itself and what its relation is to the world coincides with the question, *What is the ultimate purpose of the world?* This question implies that the purpose is to be actualized and realized. Two things, then, must be considered: first, the content of this ultimate purpose, the determination as such, and, secondly, its realization.

To begin with, we must note that world history goes on within the realm of Spirit. The term "world" includes both physical and psychical nature. Physical nature does play a part in world history, and from the very beginning we shall draw attention to the fundamental natural relations thus involved. But Spirit, and the course of its development, is the substance of history. We must not contemplate nature as a rational system in itself, in its own particular domain, but only in its relation to Spirit.

[*After the creation of nature appears Man. He constitutes the antithesis to the natural world; he is the being that lifts itself up to the second world. We have in our universal consciousness two realms, the realm of Nature and the realm of Spirit. The realm of Spirit consists in what is produced by man. One may have all sorts of ideas about the Kingdom of God; but it is always a realm of Spirit to be realized and brought about in man.*

The realm of Spirit is all-comprehensive; it includes everything that ever has interested or ever will interest man. Man is active in it; whatever he does, he is the creature within which the Spirit works. Hence it is of interest, in the course of history, to learn to know spiritual nature in its existence, that is, the point where Spirit and Nature unite, namely,

20

*human nature. In speaking of human nature we mean some-
thing permanent. The concept of human nature must fit all
men and all ages, past and present. This universal concept
may suffer infinite modifications; but actually the universal
is one and the same essence in its most various modifications.
Thinking reflection disregards the variations and adheres to
the universal, which under all circumstances is active in the
same manner and shows itself in the same interest. The universal type appears even in what seems to deviate from it most
strongly; in the most distorted figure we can still discern
the human. . . .*

*This kind of reflection abstracts from the content, the pur-
pose of human activity. . . . But the cultured human mind
cannot help making distinctions between inclinations and desires as they manifest themselves in small circumstances and
as they appear in the struggle of world-wide historical interests. Here appears an objective interest, which impresses us in
two aspects, that of the universal aim and that of the individual who represents this aim. It is this which makes history so
fascinating. These are the aims and individuals whose loss and
decline we mourn. When we have before us the struggle of
the Greeks against the Persians or Alexander's mighty domin-
ion, we know very well what interests us. We want to see the
Greeks saved from barbarism, we want the Athenian state preserved, and we are interested in the ruler under whose leader-
ship the Greeks subjugated Asia. If it were only a matter of
human passion, we would not feel any loss in imagining that
Alexander would have failed in his enterprise. We could very
well content ourselves in seeing here a mere play of passions,
but we would not feel satisfied. We have here a substantial,
an objective interest. . . .*

*In contemplating world history we must thus consider its
ultimate purpose. This ultimate purpose is what is willed in
the world itself. We know of God that He is the most perfect;
He can will only Himself and what is like Him. God and
the nature of His will are one and the same; these we call,
philosophically, the Idea. Hence, it is the Idea in general,*

in its manifestation as human spirit, which we have to contemplate. More precisely, it is the idea of human freedom. The purest form in which the Idea manifests itself is Thought itself. In this aspect the Idea is treated in Logic. Another form is that of physical Nature.[1] *The third form, finally, is that of Spirit in general.*] Spirit, on the stage on which we observe it, that of world history, is in its most concrete reality. But nevertheless—or rather in order to understand also the general idea of this concrete existence of Spirit—we must set forth, first, some general definition of the *nature of Spirit.* But this can only be done here as a mere assertion; this is not the place to develop the idea of Spirit through philosophical speculation. As was mentioned above, what can be said in an introduction can be taken only historically—as an assumption to be explained and proved elsewhere or to be verified by the science of history itself.

We have therefore to indicate here:

(1) The abstract characteristics of the nature of Spirit.

(2) The means Spirit uses in order to realize its Idea.

(3) The form which the complete realization of Spirit assumes in existence—the State.

1. THE IDEA OF FREEDOM

The nature of Spirit may be understood by a glance at its direct opposite—Matter. The essence of matter is gravity, the essence of Spirit—its substance—is Freedom. It is immediately plausible to everyone that, among other properties, Spirit also possesses Freedom. But philosophy teaches us that *all* the properties of Spirit exist only through Freedom. All are but means of attaining Freedom; all seek and produce this and this alone. It is an insight of speculative philosophy that Freedom is the sole truth of Spirit. Matter possesses gravity by virtue of its tendency toward a central point; it is essentially

[1] In this aspect the Idea is treated in the Philosophy of Nature.

composite, consisting of parts that exclude each other. It seeks
its unity and thereby its own abolition; it seeks its opposite.[2]
If it would attain this it would be matter no longer, but would
have perished. It strives toward ideality, for in unity it exists
ideally. Spirit, on the contrary, is that which has its center in
itself. It does not have unity outside of itself but has found it;
it is in itself and with itself. Matter has its substance outside
of itself; Spirit is Being-within-itself (self-contained existence).
But this, precisely, is Freedom. For when I am dependent, I
refer myself to something else which I am not; I cannot exist
independently of something external. I am free when I am
within myself. This self-contained existence of Spirit is self-
consciousness, consciousness of self.

Two things must be distinguished in consciousness, first,
that I know and, secondly, *what* I know. In self-consciousness
the two coincide, for Spirit knows itself. It is the judgment of
its own nature and, at the same time, the operation of coming
to itself, to produce itself, to make itself (actually) into that
which it is in itself (potentially). Following this abstract
definition it may be said that world history is the exhibition
of spirit striving to attain knowledge of its own nature. As the
germ bears in itself the whole nature of the tree, the taste
and shape of its fruit, so also the first traces of Spirit vir-
tually contain the whole of history. Orientals do not yet
know that Spirit—Man as such—is free. And because they
do not know it, they are not free. They only know that *one*
is free; but for this very reason such freedom is mere caprice,
ferocity, dullness of passion, or, perhaps, softness and tame-
ness of desire—which again is nothing but an accident of
nature and thus, again, caprice. This *one* is therefore only
a despot, not a free man. The consciousness of freedom first
arose among the Greeks, and therefore they were free. But
they, and the Romans likewise, only knew that some are free—
not man as such. This not even Plato and Aristotle knew.
For this reason the Greeks not only had slavery, upon which
was based their whole life and the maintenance of their splen-

[2] See *Encyklopädie der philosophischen Wissenschaften*, par. 262.

did liberty, but their freedom itself was partly an accidental, transient, and limited flowering and partly a severe thralldom of human nature. Only the Germanic peoples came, through Christianity, to realize that man as man is free and that freedom of Spirit is the very essence of man's nature. This realization first arose in religion, in the innermost region of spirit; [3] but to introduce it in the secular world was a further task which could only be solved and fulfilled by a long and severe effort of civilization. Thus slavery did not cease immediately with the acceptance of the Christian religion. Liberty did not suddenly predominate in states nor reason in governments and constitutions. The application of the principle to secular conditions, the thorough molding and interpenetration of the secular world by it, is precisely the long process of history. I have already drawn attention to this distinction between a principle as such and its application, its introduction and execution in the actuality of life and spirit. This is a fundamental fact in our science and must be kept constantly in mind. Just as we noted it in the Christian principle of self-consciousness and freedom, so it shows itself in the principle of freedom in general. World history is the progress of the consciousness of freedom—a progress whose necessity we have to investigate.

The preliminary statement given above of the various grades in the consciousness of freedom—that the Orientals knew only that *one* is free, the Greeks and Romans that *some* are free, while we know that *all* men absolutely, that is, as men, are free—is at the same time the natural division of world history and the manner in which we shall treat it. But this is only mentioned in passing; first, we must explain some other concepts.

We have established Spirit's consciousness of its freedom, and thereby the actualization of this Freedom as the final purpose of the world. For the spiritual world is the substance of reality, and the physical world remains subordinate

[3] Of the Jewish people; see *Philosophy of World History*, Part III, Section III, Ch. 2.

to it, or, in terms of speculative philosophy, has no truth compared with the former. But the term "freedom," without further qualification, is indefinite and infinitely ambiguous. Being the highest concept, it is liable to an infinity of misunderstandings, confusions, and errors and may give rise to all possible kinds of extravagances. All this has never been more clearly known and experienced than today. Yet for the time being we must content ourselves with this general, as yet undefined term. Attention was also drawn to the importance of the infinite difference between the principle, as that which so far is only in itself, and that which is real. At the same time, it is Freedom in itself that comprises within itself the infinite necessity of bringing itself to consciousness and thereby, since knowledge about itself is its very nature, to reality. Freedom is itself its own object of attainment and the sole purpose of Spirit. It is the ultimate purpose toward which all world history has continually aimed. To this end all the sacrifices have been offered on the vast altar of the earth throughout the long lapse of ages. Freedom alone is the purpose which realizes and fulfills itself, the only enduring pole in the change of events and conditions, the only truly efficient principle that pervades the whole. This final aim is God's purpose with the world. But God is the absolutely perfect Being and can, therefore, will nothing but Himself, His own will. The nature of His own will, His own nature, is what we here call the Idea of freedom. Thus we translate the language of religion into that of philosophy. Our next question then is: what are the means the Idea uses for its realization? This is the second point that we have to consider.

2. THE MEANS OF REALIZATION *of the Idea*

(a) THE IDEA AND THE INDIVIDUAL

The question of the *means* whereby Freedom develops itself into a world leads us directly to the phenomenon of history. Although Freedom as such is primarily an internal idea, the means it uses are the external phenomena which in history present themselves directly before our eyes. The first glance at history convinces us that the actions of men spring from their needs, their passions, their interests, their characters, and their talents. Indeed, it appears as if in this drama of activities these needs, passions, and interests are the sole springs of action and the main efficient cause. It is true that this drama involves also universal purposes, benevolence, or noble patriotism. But such virtues and aims are insignificant on the broad canvas of history. We may, perhaps, see the ideal of Reason actualized in those who adopt such aims and in the spheres of their influence; but their number is small in proportion to the mass of the human race and their influence accordingly limited. Passions, private aims, and the satisfaction of selfish desires are, on the contrary, tremendous springs of action. Their power lies in the fact that they respect none of the limitations which law and morality would impose on them; and that these natural impulses are closer to the core of human nature than the artificial and troublesome discipline that tends toward order, self-restraint, law, and morality.

When we contemplate this display of passions and the consequences of their violence, the unreason which is associated not only with them, but even—rather we might say *especially* —with *good* designs and righteous aims; when we see arising therefrom the evil, the vice, the ruin that has befallen the most flourishing kingdoms which the mind of man ever created, we can hardly avoid being filled with sorrow at this universal taint of corruption. And since this decay is not the work of mere nature, but of human will, our reflections may well lead us to a moral sadness, a revolt of the good will (spirit) —if indeed it has a place within us. Without rhetorical exaggeration, a simple, truthful account of the miseries that have overwhelmed the noblest of nations and polities and the finest exemplars of private virtue forms a most fearful picture and excites emotions of the profoundest and most hopeless sadness, counter-balanced by no consoling result. We can endure it and strengthen ourselves against it only by thinking that this is the way it had to be—it is fate; nothing can be done. And at last, out of the boredom with which this sorrowful reflection threatens us, we draw back into the vitality of the present, into our aims and interests of the moment; we retreat, in short, into the selfishness that stands on the quiet shore and thence enjoys in safety the distant spectacle of wreckage and confusion.

But in contemplating history as the slaughter-bench at which the happiness of peoples, the wisdom of states, and the virtue of individuals have been sacrificed, a question necessarily arises: To what principle, to what final purpose, have these monstrous sacrifices been offered?

From here one usually proceeds to the starting point of our investigation: the events which make up this picture of gloomy emotion and thoughtful reflection are only the means for realizing the essential destiny, the absolute and final purpose, or, what amounts to the same thing, the true result of world history. We have all along purposely eschewed that method of reflection which ascends from this scene of particulars to general principles. Besides, it is not in the interest of such sentimental reflections really to rise above these depressing emotions and to solve the mysteries of Providence presented in such contemplations. It is rather their nature to dwell melancholically on the empty and fruitless sublimities of their negative result. For this reason we return to our original point of view. What we shall have to say about it will also answer the questions put to us by this panorama of history.

The first thing we notice—something which has been stressed more than once before but which cannot be repeated too often, for it belongs to the central point of our inquiry—is the merely general and abstract nature of what we call principle, final purpose, destiny, or the nature and concept of Spirit. A principle, a law is something implicit, which as such, however true in itself, is not completely real (actual). Purposes, principles, and the like, are at first in our thoughts, our inner intention. They are not yet in reality. That which is in itself is a possibility, a faculty. It has not yet emerged out of its implicitness into existence. A second element must be added for it to become reality, namely, activity, actualization. The principle of this is the will, man's activity in general. It is only through this activity that the concept and its implicit ("being-in-themselves") determinations can be realized, actualized; for of themselves they have no immediate efficacy. The activity which puts them in operation and in existence is the need, the instinct, the inclination, and passion of man. When I have an idea I am greatly interested in transforming it into action, into actuality. In its realization through my participation I want to find my own satisfaction. A purpose for which I shall be active must in some way be my purpose; I must thereby satisfy my own desires, even though it may have ever so many aspects which do not concern me. This is the infinite right of the individual to find itself satisfied in its activity and labor. If men are to be interested in anything they must have "their heart" in it. Their feelings of self-importance must be satisfied. But here a misunderstanding must be avoided. To say that an individual "has an interest" in something is justly regarded as a reproach or blame; we imply that he seeks only his private advantage. Indeed, the blame implies not only his disregard of the common interest, but his taking advantage of it and even his sacrificing it to his own interest. Yet, he who is active for a cause is not simply "interested," but "interested *in it*." Language faithfully expresses this distinction. Nothing therefore happens, nothing is accomplished, unless those concerned with an issue find their own satisfaction in it. They are particular individuals; they have their special needs, instincts, and interests. They have their own particular desires and volitions, their own insight and conviction, or at least their own attitude and opinion, once the aspirations to reflect, understand, and reason have been awakened. Therefore people demand that a cause for which they should be active accord with their ideas. And they expect their opinion—concerning its goodness, justice, advantage, profit—to be taken into account. This is of particular importance today when people are moved to support a cause not by faith in other people's authority, but rather on the basis of their own independent judgment and conviction.

We assert then that nothing has been accomplished without an interest on the part of those who brought it about. And if "interest" be called "passion"—because the whole individuality is concentrating all its desires and powers, with every fiber of volition, to the neglect of all other actual or possible interests and aims, on one object—we may then affirm without qualification that *nothing great in the world* has been accomplished without passion.

Two elements therefore enter into our investigation: first, the Idea, secondly, the complex of human passions; the one the warp, the other the woof of the vast tapestry of world history. Their contact and concrete union constitutes moral liberty in the state. We have already spoken of the Idea of freedom as the essence of Spirit and absolutely final purpose of history. Passion is regarded as something wrong, something more or less evil; man is not supposed to have passions. "Passion," it is true, is not quite the right word for what I wish to express. I mean here nothing more than human activity resulting from private interest, from special or, if you will, self-seeking designs—with this qualification: that the whole energy of will and character is devoted to the attainment of one aim and that other interests or possible aims, indeed everything else, is sacrificed to this aim. This particular objective is so bound up with the person's will that it alone and entirely determines its direction and is inseparable from it. It is that which makes the person what he is. For a person is a specific existence. He is not man in general—such a thing does not exist—but a particular human being. The term "character" also expresses this uniqueness of will and intelligence. But character comprises all individual features whatever—the way in which a person conducts himself in his private and other relations. It does not connote this individuality itself in its practical and active phase. I shall therefore use the term "passion" to mean the particularity of a character insofar as its individual volitions not only have a particular content but also supply the impelling and actuating force for deeds of universal scope. Passion is thus the subjective and therefore the formal aspect of energy, will, and activity, whose content and aim are at this point still undetermined. And a similar relation exists between individual conviction, insight, and conscience, on the one hand, and their content, on the other. If someone wants to decide whether my conviction and passion are true and substantial, he must consider the *content* of my conviction and the *aim* of my passion. Conversely, if they are true and substantial, they cannot help but attain actual existence.

From this comment on the second essential element in the historical embodiment of an aim, we infer—considering for a moment the institution of the state—that a state is then well constituted and internally vigorous when the private interest of its citizens is one with the common interest of the state, and the one finds gratification and realization in the other—a most important proposition. But in a state many institutions are necessary—inventions, appropriate arrangements, accompanied by long intellectual struggles in order to find out what is really appropriate, as well as struggles with private interests and passions, which must be harmonized in difficult and tedious discipline. When a state reaches this harmony, it has reached the period of its bloom, its excellence, its power and prosperity. But world history does not begin with any conscious aim, as do the *particular* circles of men. Already the simple instinct of living together contains the conscious purpose of securing life and property; once this primal society has been established, the purpose expands. But world history begins its *general* aim—to realize the idea of Spirit—only in an implicit form (*an sich*), namely, as Nature—as an innermost, unconscious instinct. And the whole business of history, as already observed, is to bring it into consciousness. Thus, appearing in the form of nature, of natural will, what we have called the subjective side is immediate, actual existence (*für sich*) : need, instinct, passion, private interest, even opinion and subjective representation. These vast congeries of volitions, interests, and activities constitute the tools and means of the World Spirit for attaining its purpose, bringing it to consciousness, and realizing it. And this purpose is none other than finding itself—coming to itself—and contemplating itself in concrete actuality. But one may indeed question whether those manifestations of vitality on the part of individuals and peoples in which they seek and satisfy their own purposes are, at the same time, the means and tools of a higher and broader purpose of which they know nothing, which they realize unconsciously. This purpose has been questioned, and in every variety of form denied, decried, and denounced as mere dreaming and "philosophy." On this point, however, I announced my view at the very outset, and asserted our hypothesis—which eventually will appear as the result of our investigation—namely, that Reason governs the world and has consequently governed its history. In relation to this Reason, which is universal and substantial, in and for itself, all else is subordinate, subservient, and the means for its actualization. Moreover, this Reason is immanent in historical existence and reaches its own perfection in and through this existence. The union of the abstract universal, existing in and for itself, with the particular or subjective, and the fact that this union alone constitutes truth are a matter of speculative philosophy which, in this general form, is treated in logic. But in its historical development [*the subjective side, consciousness, is not yet able to know what is*] the abstract final aim of history, the idea of Spirit, for it is then itself in process and incomplete. The idea of Spirit is not yet its distinct object of desire and interest. Thus desire is still unconscious of its purpose; yet it already exists in the particular purposes and realizes itself through them. The problem concerning the union of the general and the subjective may also be raised under the form of the union of freedom and necessity. We consider the immanent development of the Spirit, existing in and for itself, as necessary, while we refer to freedom the interests contained in men's conscious volitions. Since, as was said, the speculative, that is, the conceptual aspect of this connection belongs to logic, it would be out of place to analyze it here. But the chief and cardinal points may be mentioned.

In philosophy we show that the Idea proceeds to its infinite antithesis. . . . [*The Idea has within itself the determination of its self-consciousness, of activity. Thus it is God's own eternal life, as it was, so to speak, before the creation of the world, (the) logical connection (of all things). It still lacks at this point the form of being which is actuality. It still is the universal, the immanent, the represented. The second stage begins when the Idea satisfies the contrast which originally is only ideally in it and posits the difference between itself in its free universal mode, in which it remains within itself, and itself as purely abstract reflection in itself. In thus stepping over to one side (in order to be object of reflection) the Idea sets the other side as formal actuality (Fürsichsein), as formal freedom, as abstract unity of self-consciousness, as infinite reflection in itself, and as infinite negativity (antithesis).[4] Thus it becomes Ego, which, as an atom (indivisible), opposes itself to all content and thus is the most complete antithesis—the antithesis, namely, of the whole plenitude of the Idea. The absolute Idea is thus, on the one hand, substantial fullness of content and, on the other hand, abstract free volition. God and universe have separated, and set each other as opposites. Consciousness, the Ego, has a being such that the other (everything else) is for it (its object). In developing this train of thought one arrives at the creation of free spirits, the world, and so on. The absolute antithesis, the atom (i.e., the Ego), which at the same time is a manifold (of contents of consciousness), is finiteness itself. It is for itself (in actuality) merely exclusion of its antithesis (the absolute Idea). It is its limit and barrier. Thus it is the Absolute itself become finite. Reflection in itself, individual self-consciousness, is the antithesis of the absolute Idea and hence the Idea in absolute finiteness. This finitude, the acme of freedom, this formal knowledge—*

---

[4] Note this fivefold development of the Idea. It implies what follows.

*when referred to the glory of God as to the absolute Idea
which recognizes what ought to be—is the soil on which the
spiritual element of knowledge as such is falling; thus it constitutes the absolute aspect of its actuality, though it remains
merely formal.*]

To comprehend the absolute connection of this opposition
is the profound task of metaphysics. [*The Divine, and hence
religion, exists for the Ego, and likewise also the world in
general, that is, the universal totality of finite existence, exists
for the Ego. The Ego, in this relation, is itself its own finiteness and comprehends itself as finite. Thus it is the viewpoint
of finite purposes, of mere appearance. (At the same time it
is particularity of consciousness.) Consciousness in itself, freedom abstractly considered, is the formal aspect of the activity
of the absolute Idea. This self-consciousness, first of all, wills
itself in general and, secondly, wills itself in every particular.
This self-knowing subjectivity projects itself into all objectivity. This constitutes the Ego's certainty of its own existence.
Inasmuch as this subjectivity has no other content, it must be
called the rational desire—just as piety is nothing but the
desire for the subject's salvation. The Ego thus wills itself
primarily not as conscious but as finite in its immediacy. This
is the sphere of its phenomenality. It wills itself in its particularity. At this point we find the passions, where individuality realizes its particularity. If it succeeds in thus realizing
its finiteness, it doubles itself (its potential finiteness becomes
actual finiteness). Through this reconciliation of the atom and
its othernesses individuals are what we call happy, for happy
is he who is in harmony with himself. One may contemplate
history from the point of view of happiness.*] But actually
history is not the soil of happiness. The periods of happiness
are blank pages in it. [*There is, it is true, satisfaction in world
history. But it is not the kind that is called happiness, for it
is satisfaction of purposes that are above particular interests.
Purposes that are relevant for world history must be grasped
in abstract volition and with energy. The world-historical individuals who have pursued such purposes have satisfied*

themselves, it is true, but they did not want to be happy.[5]

This element of abstract action] is to be regarded as the bond, the middle term, between the universal Idea, which reposes in the inner recesses of Spirit, and the external world. [*It is that which carries the Idea from its immanence into its external state. Universality, in being externalized, is at the same time made particular. The immanent by itself would be dead, abstract. Through action it becomes existent. Conversely, activity elevates (the) empty objectivity (of nature) to be the appearance of the essence which is in and for itself.*]

(b) THE INDIVIDUAL AS SUBJECT OF HISTORY

[*In world history we deal with the Idea as it manifests itself in the element of human will, of human freedom. . . . Objectively seen, the Idea and the particular individual stand in the great opposition of Necessity and Freedom—the struggle of man against fate. But we take necessity not as the external necessity of fate, but as that of the divine Idea. The question then is: How is this high Idea to be united with human freedom? The will of the individual is free when it can posit abstractly, absolutely, and in and for itself that which it wills. How then can the universal, the rational in general, be determinant in history? This contradiction cannot be clarified here in complete detail. But think of the following:*

The flame consumes the air; it is nourished by wood. The air is the sole condition for the growing of trees. In the wood's endeavor to consume the air through fire, it fights against itself and against its own source. And yet oxygen continues in the air and the trees do not cease to grow green. So also when someone starts building a house, his decision to do so is freely made. But all the elements must help. And yet the house is being built to protect man against the elements. Hence the elements are here used against themselves. But the general

---

[5] They wanted to be great. Greatness is satisfaction in large situations, happiness satisfaction in small situations. Cf. Introduction, p. xxviii.

law of nature is not disturbed thereby.] The building of a
house is, in the first instance, a subjective aim and design. On
the other hand we have, as means, the several substances required for the work—iron, wood, stones. The elements are
used in preparing this material: fire to melt the iron, wind
to blow the fire, water to set wheels in motion in order to cut
the wood, etc. The result is that the wind, which has helped
to build the house, is shut out by the house; so also are the
violence of rains and floods and the destructive powers of fire,
so far as the house is made fire-proof. The stones and beams
obey the law of gravity and press downwards so that the high
walls are held up. Thus the elements are made use of in accordance with their nature and cooperate for a product by
which they become constrained. In a similar way the passions
of men satisfy themselves; they develop themselves and their
purposes in accordance with their natural destination and
produce the edifice of human society. Thus they fortify a
structure for law and order *against* themselves. [*Thus the passions are by no means always opposed to morality but actualize the universal. As far as their own morality is concerned,
it is true, they strive to realize their own interests. Thus they*
appear *bad and self-seeking. But action is always individual;
it is always I who act. It is my purpose which I want to fulfill.
This purpose may be a good one, a universal aim; on the
other hand, the interest may be a particular, a private one.
This does not mean that it is necessarily opposed to the universal good. On the contrary, the universal must be actualized
through the particular.*]

This connection implies that human actions in history produce additional results, beyond their immediate purpose and
attainment, beyond their immediate knowledge and desire.
They gratify their own interests; but something more is
thereby accomplished, which is latent in the action though
not present in their consciousness and not included in their
design. An analogous example is offered in the case of a man
who, thirsting for revenge perhaps justly to redress an unjust
injury, sets fire to another man's house. The deed immediately

establishes a train of circumstances not directly connected with it, taken in itself. In itself it consists in merely presenting a small flame to a small portion of a beam. Events not involved in that simple act follow of themselves. The part of the beam which was set afire is connected with its remote portions; the beam itself is united with the woodwork of the house and this with other houses, and a wide conflagration ensues. It destroys the goods and chattels of many other persons besides those of the original victim and may even cost their lives. This lay neither in the deed itself, nor in the design of the man who committed it. But the action has a further general bearing. In the design of the doer it was only revenge executed against an individual through the destruction of his property. But it is moreover a crime, and that involves punishment. All this may not have been present to the mind of the perpetrator, still less in his intention; but his deed itself, the general principles that it calls into play, its substantial content, entail it. By this example I wish only to impress on you the consideration that in a simple act something further may be implicated than lies in the intention and consciousness of the agent. The example before us involves, however, this additional consideration, that the substance of the act—consequently we may say the act itself—recoils upon the perpetrator, reacts upon him and destroys him.

This union of the two extremes—the embodiment of a general idea in immediate actuality and the elevation of a particularity into universal truth—comes about under the condition of the diversity and mutual indifference of the two extremes. The human agents have before them limited aims, special interests. But they are also intelligent, thinking beings. Their purposes are interwoven with general and essential considerations of law, the good, duty, etc. For mere desire, volition in its raw and savage form, falls outside the scene and sphere of world history. These general considerations, which at the same time form norms for directing purposes and actions, have a definite content. For such empty abstractions as "good for its own sake" have no place in living actuality.

If men are to act, they must not only intend the good but must know whether this or that particular course is good. What special course of action is good or not, right or wrong, is determined, for the ordinary circumstances of private life, by the laws and customs of a state. It is not too difficult to know them. [*It is part of the freedom in the state . . . that no apportionment in castes determines to which business an individual should dedicate himself. The morality of the individual, then, consists in his fulfilling the duties of his social position. And it is an easy matter to know what these duties are; they are determined by this position. The substantial content of such a relationship, its rationale, is known. It is, precisely, what is called duty. To investigate the content of duty is unnecessary speculation; in the tendency to regard the moral as a difficult problem, we rather sense the desire to get rid of one's duties.*] Each individual has his position; he knows, on the whole, what a lawful and honorable course of conduct is. To assert in ordinary private relations that it is difficult to choose the right and good, and to regard it as mark of an exalted morality to find difficulties and raise scruples on that score indicates an evil and perverse will. It indicates a will that seeks to evade obvious duties or, at least, a petty will that gives its mind too little to do. The mind, then, in idle reflection, busies itself with itself and indulges in moral smugness.

[*The essence of a moral relation lies in the substantial nature that duty indicates. Thus, the nature of the relation between children and parents simply lies in the duty to behave accordingly. Or, to mention a legal relationship, if I owe money to someone, I just have to act according to law and the nature of the relation and return the money. There is nothing problematic in all this. The basis of duty is the civil life: the individuals have their assigned business and hence their assigned duties. Their morality consists in acting accordingly. . . .*

But each individual is also the child of a people at a definite stage of its development. One cannot skip over the spirit of his people any more than one can skip over the earth. The earth is the center of gravity; a body imagined as leaving this center can only be imagined as exploding into the air. So it is with an individual. But only through his own effort can he be in harmony with his substance; he must bring the will demanded by his people to his own consciousness, to articulation. The individual does not invent his own content; he is what he is by acting out the universal as his own content.

This universal content everyone must activate within himself. Through this activity he maintains the whole of ethical life. But there is another element active in history which does bring about just this difficulty of acting according to ethical norms. We saw earlier, in the discussion of the dialectic of the Idea, where this universal content originates. It cannot originate within the ethical community. There particular events may occur that violate its determinate universality, such as vice, fraud, and the like, which are suppressed. But a moral whole, as such, is limited. It must have above it a higher universality, which makes it disunited in itself. The transition from one spiritual pattern to the next is just this, that the former moral whole, in itself a universal, through being thought (in terms of the higher universal), is abolished as a particular.[6] The later universal, so to speak, the next higher genus of the preceding species, is potentially but not yet actually present in the preceding one. This makes all existing reality unstable and disunited.

In the course of history two factors are important. One is the preservation of a people, a state, of the well-ordered spheres of life. This is the activity of individuals participating in the common effort and helping to bring about its particular manifestations. It is the preservation of ethical life. The other important factor, however, is the decline of a state. The existence of a national spirit is broken when it has used up and exhausted itself. World history, the World Spirit, continues on its course. We cannot deal here with the position of the individuals within the moral whole and their moral conduct and duty. We are concerned with the Spirit's develop-

[6] For it is elevated into the universal.

ment, its progression and ascent to an ever higher concept of itself. But this development is connected with the degradation, destruction, annihilation of the preceding mode of actuality which the concept of the Spirit had evolved. This is the result, on the one hand, of the inner development of the Idea and, on the other, of the activity of individuals, who are its agents and bring about its actualization.] It is at this point that appear those momentous collisions between existing, acknowledged duties, laws, and rights and those possibilities which are adverse to this system, violate it, and even destroy its foundations and existence. Their tenor may nevertheless seem good, on the whole advantageous—yes, even indispensable and necessary. These possibilities now become historical fact; they involve a universal of an order different from that upon which depends the permanence of a people or a state. This universal is an essential phase in the development of the creating Idea, of truth striving and urging toward itself. The historical men, *world-historical individuals*, are those [*who grasp just such a higher universal, make it their own purpose, and realize this purpose in accordance with the higher law of the spirit*].

Caesar was such a man. Before reaching his position of superiority he was in danger of losing his place of equality with the other leaders of Rome. He was about to succumb to those who were just becoming his enemies. These enemies, who at the same time pursued their own personal interests, had on their side the formal constitution of Rome and the power of legal appearance. Caesar fought to keep his position, honor, and safety. But victory over his enemies, who held the power over all the Roman provinces, became at the same time conquest of the entire empire. Thus Caesar, without changing the form of the constitution, became the sole ruler of the state. In accomplishing his originally negative purpose—the autocracy over Rome—he at the same time fulfilled the necessary historical destiny of Rome and the world. Thus he was motivated not only by his own private interest, but acted instinctively to bring to pass that which the times required. It is the same with all great historical individuals: their own particular purposes contain the substantial will of the World Spirit. They must be called "heroes," insofar as they have derived their purpose and vocation not from the calm, regular course of things, sanctioned by the existing order, but from a secret source whose content is still hidden and has not yet broken through into existence. The source of their actions is the inner spirit, still hidden beneath the surface but already knocking against the outer world as against a shell, in order, finally, to burst forth and break it into pieces; for it is a kernel different from that which belongs to the shell. They are men, therefore, who appear to draw the impulses of their lives from themselves. Their deeds have produced a condition of things and a complex of historical relations that appear to be their own interest and their own work.

Such individuals have no consciousness of the Idea as such. They are practical and political men. But at the same time they are thinkers with insight into what is needed and timely. They see the very truth of their age and their world, the next genus, so to speak, which is already formed in the womb of time. It is theirs to know this new universal, the necessary next stage of their world, to make it their own aim and put all their energy into it. The world-historical persons, the heroes of their age, must therefore be recognized as its seers— their words and deeds are the best of the age.[7] Great men have worked for their own satisfaction and not that of others. Whatever prudent designs and well-meant counsels they might have gotten from others would have been limited and inappropriate under the circumstances. For it is they who knew best and from whom the others eventually learned and with whom they agreed or, at least, complied. For Spirit, in taking this new historical step, is the innermost soul of all individuals—but in a state of unconsciousness, which the great men arouse to consciousness. For this reason their fellow men

---

[7] This seems to imply that insofar as they only bring about the destruction of the old, the antithesis to the thesis, without synthesis, their words and actions are the worst of their age.

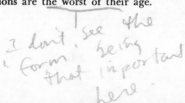

follow these soul-leaders, [*they stream to their banner*]. For they feel the irresistible power of their own spirit embodied in them.

Let us now cast a look at the fate of these world-historical individuals. [*They were fortunate in being the agents of a purpose which constitutes a step in the progress of the universal Spirit. But as individuals distinguished from their substantial aim, they were not what is commonly called happy, nor did they want to be.*[8] *They wanted to achieve their aim, and they achieved it by their toil and labor. They succeeded in finding their satisfaction in bringing about their purpose, the universal purpose. With such a grand aim they had the boldness to challenge all the opinions of men.*] Thus they attained no calm enjoyment. Their whole life was labor and trouble, their whole being was in their passion. Once their objective is attained, they fall off like empty hulls from the kernel. They die early like Alexander, they are murdered like Caesar, transported to Saint Helena like Napoleon. This awful fact, that historical men were not what is called happy—for only private life in its manifold external circumstances can be "happy"—may serve as a consolation for those people who need it, the envious ones who cannot tolerate greatness and eminence. They strive to criticize the great and belittle greatness. Thus in modern times it has been demonstrated *ad nauseam* that princes are generally unhappy on their thrones. For this reason one does not begrudge them their position and finds it tolerable that *they* rather than oneself sit on the throne. The free man, however, is not envious, but gladly recognizes what is great and exalted and rejoices in its existence. . . . [*But to such great men attaches a whole train of envy, which tries to demonstrate that their passion is a vice. One can indeed apply the term "passion" to the phenomenon of the great men and can judge them morally by saying that passion had driven them. They were indeed men of passion: they had the passion of their conviction and put their whole character, genius, and energy into it. Here, then, what is neces-*

[8] Cf. above, p. 34, note 5.

*sary in and for itself appears in the form of passion. These
great men seem only to follow their passion and their arbitrary wills. But what they pursue is the universal; that alone
is their pathos. The passion precisely has been the energy of
their ego; without it they would not have been able to achieve
anything.*

*In this way the purpose of passion and the purpose of the
Idea are one and the same. Passion is the absolute unity of
individual character and the universal. It is something almost
animalic how the spirit in its subjective particularity here
becomes identified with the Idea. . . .*

*By fulfilling their own great purpose in accordance with the
necessity of the universal Spirit, these world-historical men
also satisfy themselves. These two things belong inseparably
together: the cause and its hero. They must both be satisfied. . . . It is psychological pedantry to make a separation
and, by giving passion the name of addiction, to suspect the
morality of these men. By saying they acted only from morbid
craving, one presents the consequences of their actions as their
purposes and degrades the actions themselves to means.]* Alexander of Macedon partly conquered Greece and then Asia;
it is said, therefore, that he craved conquest, and as proof it is
offered that he did things which resulted in fame. What
schoolmaster has not demonstrated that Alexander the Great
and Julius Caesar were driven by such passions and were, consequently, immoral? From which it immediately follows that
he, the schoolmaster, is a better man than they because he
has no such passions, and proves it by the fact that he has not
conquered Asia nor vanquished Darius and Porus, but enjoys
life and allows others to enjoy it too. These psychologists are
particularly fond of contemplating those peculiarities that
belong to great historical figures as private persons. Man must
eat and drink; he has relations with friends and acquaintances;
he has emotions and fits of temper. "No man is a hero to his
valet de chambre," is a well-known proverb; I have added—
and Goethe repeated it two years later—"but not because the

former is no hero, but because the latter is a valet." [9] He takes off the hero's boots, helps him into bed, knows that he prefers champagne, and the like. Historical personages fare badly in historical literature when served by such psychological valets. These attendants degrade them to their own level, or rather a few degrees below the level of their own morality, these exquisite discerners of spirits. Homer's Thersites, who abuses the kings, is a standing figure for all times. Not in every age, it is true, does he get blows—that is, beating with a solid cudgel—as in the Homeric one. But his envy, his egotism, is the thorn that he has to carry in his flesh; and the undying worm that gnaws him is the tormenting thought that his excellent intentions and criticisms get absolutely no result in the world. One may be allowed a certain glee over Thersites' fate.

A world-historical individual is not so sober as to adjust his ambition to circumstances; nor is he very considerate. He is devoted, come what may, to one purpose. Therefore such men may treat other great and even sacred interests inconsiderately—a conduct which indeed subjects them to moral reprehension. But so mighty a figure must trample down many an innocent flower, crush to pieces many things in its path.

(c) THE INDIVIDUAL AS OBJECT OF HISTORY

The special interest of passion is thus inseparable from the actualization of the universal; for the universal results from the particular and definite and its negation. [*The particular has its own role to play in world history; it is finite and must, as such, perish.*] It is the particular which exhausts itself in the struggle and part of which is destroyed. [*But the universal results precisely from this struggle, from the destruction of the particular.*] It is not the general Idea that involves itself in opposition and combat and exposes itself to danger; it remains in the background, untouched and uninjured. This may be

[9] Hegel's remark appeared in the *Phenomenology of Mind*, 1807. Goethe used it in *Elective Affinities*, 1809 (Part II, Ch. 5, "Ottilia's Diary").

called the *cunning of Reason*—that it sets the passions to work for itself, while that through which it develops itself pays the penalty and suffers the loss. For it is the phenomenal which in part is negative, in part positive. The particular in most cases is too trifling as compared with the universal; the individuals are sacrificed and abandoned. The Idea pays the tribute of existence and transience, not out of its own funds but with the passions of the individuals.

We might find it tolerable that individuals, their purposes and gratifications, are thus sacrificed, their happiness abandoned to the realm of [*natural forces and hence of*] chance to which it belongs; and that individuals in general are regarded under the category of means. Yet there is one aspect of human individuality that we must refuse to take exclusively in this light even in relation to the highest, an element which is absolutely not subordinate but exists in individuals as essentially eternal and divine. I mean morality,[10] ethics, religion. Already in discussing the role of individuals in the realization of the rational aim we said that the subjective element in them, their interests, cravings, and impulses, their views and judgments had an infinite right to be satisfied, although we regarded these as only the formal aspect of the process. In speaking of means we imagine, first of all, something external to the end which has no share in it. But actually even merely natural things, the most common lifeless objects used as means, must somehow be adapted to their purpose; they must have something in common with it. This bare external relation of mere means is the least relation human beings have to the rational purpose. In the very act of realizing it they make it the occasion of satisfying their personal desires, whose import is different from that purpose. Moreover, they share in the rational purpose itself and for that very reason are ends in themselves—not merely formally, as is the world of other living beings, whose individual life is essentially subordinate

10 Note the difference between the intrinsic morality (*Moralität*) meant here and the previously mentioned extrinsic morality of social position (*Sittlichkeit*).

to that of man and is properly used up as an instrument. Men, on the contrary, are ends in themselves in regard to the content of the end. This defines those elements which we demand to be exempt from the category of means: morality, ethics, religion.[11]

Man is an end in himself only by virtue of the divine in him—that which we designated at the outset as *Reason,* or, insofar as it has activity and power of self-determination, as *Freedom.* And we say—without entering at present into further discussion—that religiosity, morality, etc., have their foundation and source in it and are thus essentially exempt from external necessity and chance. [*But we must not forget that here we speak of morality, religiosity, etc., only insofar as they exist in individuals, hence, subject to individual freedom. In this sense, that is,*] to the extent of their freedom, individuals are responsible for the depravation and enfeeblement of morality and religion. This is the seal of the absolute and sublime destiny of man, that he knows what is good and what is evil, and that his destiny is his very ability to will either good or evil. In one word, he can be guilty—guilty not only of evil but of good, and not only concerning this or that particular matter and all that happens in and around him *(Sittlichkeit),* but also the good and evil attaching to his individual freedom *(Moralität).* The animal alone is truly innocent. It would, however, require an extensive explanation—as extensive as that of freedom itself—to avoid or refute all the misunderstandings which usually arise from the statement that the word "innocence" means ignorance of evil.

In contemplating the fate which virtue, morality, even piety have in history, we must not fall into the litany of lamentations that the good and pious often, or for the most part, fare ill in the world, while the evil and wicked prosper. By prosperity one may understand a variety of things—riches, outward honor, and the like. But in speaking of purpose in and for itself, the so-called prosperity or misfortune of this or that isolated individual cannot be regarded as an essential element

[11] Which refer to the essential nature of man as an end in himself.

in the rational order of the universe. With more reason than merely the happiness or fortunate circumstances of individuals we demand of the purpose of the world that good, moral, righteous purposes should find in and under it their satisfaction and security. What makes men morally discontented—a discontent on which they pride themselves—is that they do not find the present appropriate for the realization of aims which in their opinion are right and good—especially the ideals of political institutions of our time. They contrast things as they are with their ideal of things as they ought to be. In this case it is neither private interest nor passion that desires gratification, but reason, justice, liberty. In their name people demand their due and often are not merely discontent but rebellious against the condition of the world. To estimate such views and feelings one would have to examine the stubborn demands and dogmatic opinions in question. At no time as much as in our own have such general principles and notions been advanced with so much pretentiousness. At other times history seems to present itself as a struggle of passions. In our time, however, though passions are not wanting, history exhibits partly and predominantly a struggle of justifiable ideas and partly a struggle of passions and subjective interests under the mask of such higher pretensions. These pretensions, regarded as legitimate in the name of the supposed destiny of Reason, are thereby validated as absolute ends—in the same way as religion, morality, ethics.

As was said earlier, nothing is now more common than the complaint that the *ideals* which imagination sets up are not actualized, that these glorious dreams are destroyed by cold actuality. These ideals, which in the voyage of life founder on the rocks of hard reality, may be merely subjective to begin with and belong to the peculiarity of an individual who regards himself as supremely wise. Such ideals do not belong here. For what an individual fancies for himself in his isolation cannot be the norm for universal reality. The universal law is not designed for individuals, as such, who indeed may find themselves very much the losers. But by the term "ideal" we also understand the ideal of Reason, of the good and true. Poets, like Schiller, have painted such ideals touchingly and with strong emotion, and with the deeply melancholy conviction that they could never be actualized. In affirming, on the contrary, that the universal Reason *does* actualize itself, we have nothing to do with the empirical detail. For this can be better or worse; here chance and particularity have received authority to exercise their tremendous power. Much fault, therefore, might be found in phenomenal details. This subjective fault-finding is easy, particularly since it keeps in view only the detail and its deficiency, without understanding the universal Reason in it. In asserting good intentions for the welfare of the whole and exhibiting a semblance of good-heartedness, it can swagger about with great airs. It is easier to discover the deficiency in individuals, in states, and in Providence, than to see their real meaning. For in negative fault-finding one stands nobly and with proud mien above the matter, without penetrating into it and without comprehending its positive aspects. Age generally makes people more tolerant; youth is always discontented. For older people have a more mature judgment, which accepts even the bad, not out of mere indifference but because it has been more deeply taught by the grave experience of life. It has thus been led to the essence, the intrinsic value of the matter in question.

The insight then to which—in opposition to these ideals—philosophy should lead us is that the actual world is as it ought to be, that the truly good, the universal divine Reason is the power capable of actualizing itself. This good, this Reason, in its most concrete representation, is God. God governs the world. The actual working of His government, the carrying out of His plan is the history of the world. Philosophy strives to comprehend this plan, for only that which has been carried out according to it has reality; whatever does not accord with it is but worthless existence. Before the pure light of this divine Idea, which is no mere ideal, the illusion disappears as though the world were a crazy, inane process. Philosophy wishes to recognize the content, the reality of the divine Idea, and to justify the spurned actuality; for Reason is the comprehension of the divine work.

But then what about the atrophy, corruption, and ruin of religious, ethical, and moral purposes and social conditions in general? It must be said that essentially these purposes are infinite and eternal. But the forms that they assume may be of a limited order and consequently belong to the realm of mere nature, subject to the sway of chance. They are therefore transitory and exposed to atrophy and corruption. Religion and morality, as the universal essences in themselves, have the peculiarity of being present, conformably to their concepts and therefore truthfully, in the individual soul, although they may not be represented there fully elaborated and applied to completely developed conditions. The religiousness, the morality of a limited life—of a shepherd, a peasant—in their concentrated inward limitation to a few and quite simple circumstances of life, has infinite value. It has the same value as the religiousness and morality of a trained intellect and of an existence rich in scope of relations and activities. This inner focus, this simple region of the claims of subjective freedom—the seat of volition, resolution, and action, the abstract content of conscience, that wherein responsibility and worth of the individual are enclosed—remains untouched. It is quite shut out from the noisy din of world history, not only from its external and temporal changes but also from all alterations entailed by the absolute necessity of the concept of freedom itself.[12] In general, however, it must be noted that for whatever in the world is acclaimed as noble and glorious there is something even higher. The claim of the World Spirit rises above all special claims.

So much concerning the means which the World Spirit uses for actualizing its concept. Simply and abstractedly, it is the activity of the subjects in whom Reason is present as their substantial essence in itself, but still obscure and concealed from them. The matter becomes more complicated and diffi-

[12] But note that insofar as freedom is rational, individual conscience is in accord with it. (Cf. *Philosophy of Right,* par. 129 ff.)

cult when we regard the individuals not merely as active but, more concretely, consider the definite content of their religion and morality—features which have part in Reason and thereby in its absolute claims. Here the relation of mere means to an end disappears. The main points of this seeming difficulty with regard to the absolute purpose of Spirit have been briefly considered.

3. THE STATE

(a) THE STATE AS REALIZATION OF THE IDEA

The third point, then, concerns the end to be attained by these means, that is, the form it assumes in the realm of the actual. We have spoken of means; but the carrying out of a subjective, limited aim also requires a *material* element, either already present or to be procured or to serve this actualization. Thus the question would arise: What is the material in which the final end of Reason is to be realized? It is first of all the subjective agent itself, human desires, subjectivity in general. In human knowledge and volition, as its material basis, the rational attains existence. We have considered subjective volition with its purpose, namely, the truth of reality, insofar as moved by a great world-historical passion. As a subjective will in limited passions it is dependent; it can gratify its particular desires only within this dependence. But the subjective will has also a substantial life, a reality where it moves in the region of essential being and has the essential itself as the object of its existence. This essential being is the union of the subjective with the rational will; it is the moral whole, the *State*. It is that actuality in which the individual has and enjoys his freedom, but only as knowing, believing, and willing the universal. This must not be understood as if the subjective will of the individual attained its gratification and enjoyment through the common will and the latter were a means for it—as if the individual limited his freedom among the other individuals, so that this common limitation, the mutual constraint of all, might secure a small space of liberty for each. (This would only be negative freedom.) Rather, law, morality, the State, and they alone, are the positive reality and satisfaction of freedom. The caprice of the individual is not freedom. It is this caprice which is being limited, the license of particular desires.

The subjective will, passion, is the force which actualizes and realizes. The Idea is the interior; the State is the externally existing, genuinely moral life. It is the union of the universal and essential with the subjective will, and as such it is *Morality.* The individual who lives in this unity has a moral life, a value which consists in this substantiality alone.[13] Sophocles' Antigone says: "The divine commands are not of yesterday nor of today; no, they have an infinite existence, and no one can say whence they came." [14] The laws of ethics are not accidental, but are rationality itself. It is the end of the State to make the substantial prevail and maintain itself in the actual doings of men and in their convictions. It is the absolute interest of Reason that this moral whole exist; and herein lies the justification and merit of heroes who have founded states, no matter how crude.

[*What counts in a state is the practice of acting according to a common will and adopting universal aims. Even in the crude state there is subjection of one will under another; but this does not mean that the individual does not have a will of his own. It means that his particular will has no validity. Whims, lusts are not valid. The particularity of the will is being renounced already in such crude political formations. What counts is the common will. In thus being suppressed*

[13] Social institutions, originally extrinsic to the individual and his intrinsic morality, grow up to complete this morality in the course of their development. Their totality, the State, thus becomes itself intrinsic morality, both with respect to the individual, as completion of his intrinsic freedom, and to the World Spirit, as concretion of its universal Freedom.

[14] This seems an unfortunate reference, for Antigone *opposes* the eternal laws of the gods to the temporal commands of a state—thus making a point opposed to the one here being made by Hegel.

the individual will retires into itself. And this is the first condition necessary for the existence of the universal, the condition, namely, of knowledge, of thought—for it is thought that man has in common with the divine.[15] *It thus makes its appearance in the state. Only on this soil, that is, in the state, can art and religion exist. The objects of our considerations are peoples that have organized themselves rationally.*] In world history only those peoples that form states can come to our notice. [*One must not imagine that such organizations could appear on a desert island or in isolation. Although it is true that all great men have formed themselves in solitude, they have done so only by assimilating what the state had already created. The universal must be not only something which the individual merely intends, but which is in existence. As such it is present in the state; it is that which is valid in it. Here inwardness is at the same time actuality. It is but actuality of an external manifold, yet comprehended here in universality.*

The universal Idea manifests itself in the state. The term "manifestation" has here a meaning different from the usual one. Usually we distinguish between power (potentiality) and manifestation, as if the former were the essential, the latter the unessential or external. But no concrete determination lies as yet in the category of power itself, while where Spirit is, or the concrete concept, manifestation itself is the essential. The criterion of Spirit is its action, its active essence. Man is his own action, the sequence of his actions, that into which he has been making himself. Thus Spirit is essentially Energy; and in regard to Spirit one cannot set aside its manifestation. The manifestation of Spirit is its actual self-determination, and this is the element of its concrete nature. Spirit which does not determine itself is an abstraction of the intellect. The manifestation of Spirit is its self-determination, and it is this manifestation that we have to investigate in the form of states and individuals.

The spiritual individual, the people, insofar as it is or-

[15] This clause is restored from the first edition.

*ganized in itself, an organic whole, is what we call the State.
This designation is ambiguous in that by "state" and "constitutional law" one usually means the simple political aspect
as distinct from religion, science, and art. But when we speak
of the manifestation of the spiritual we understand the term
"state" in a more comprehensive sense, similar to the term*
Reich *(empire, realm). For us, then, a people is primarily a
spiritual individual. We do not emphasize the external aspects
but concentrate on what has been called the spirit of a people.
We mean its consciousness of itself, of its own truth, its own
essence, the spiritual powers which live and rule in it. The
universal which manifests itself in the State and is known in
it—the* form *under which everything that is, is subsumed—is
that which constitutes the* culture *of a nation. The definite*
content *which receives this universal form and is contained
in the concrete actuality of the state is the* spirit of the people. *The actual state is animated by this spirit in all its
particular affairs, wars, institutions, etc. This spiritual content
is something definite, firm, solid, completely exempt from
caprice, the particularities, the whims of individuality, of
chance. That which is subject to the latter is not the nature
of the people: it is like the dust playing over a city or a field,
which does not essentially transform it. This spiritual content
then constitutes the essence of the individual as well as that
of the people. It is the holy bond that ties the men, the spirits
together. It is one life in all, a grand object, a great purpose
and content on which depend all individual happiness and all
private decisions.] [The state does not exist for the citizens;
on the contrary, one could say that the state is the end and
they are its means. But the means-end relation is not fitting
here. For the state is not the abstract confronting the citizens;
they are parts of it, like members of an organic body, where
no member is end and none is means.]* It is the realization
of Freedom, of the absolute, final purpose, and exists for
its own sake. All the value man has, all spiritual reality, he
has only through the state. For his spiritual reality is the
knowing presence to him of his own essence, of rationality,

of its objective, immediate actuality present in and for him. Only thus is he truly a consciousness, only thus does he partake in morality, in the legal and moral life of the state. For the True is the unity of the universal and particular will. And the universal in the state is in its laws, its universal and rational provisions. The state is the divine Idea as it exists on earth.

Thus the State is the definite object of world history proper. In it freedom achieves its objectivity and lives in the enjoyment of this objectivity. For law is the objectivity of Spirit; it is will in its true form. Only the will that obeys the law is free, for it obeys itself and, being in itself, is free. In so far as the state, our country, constitutes a community of existence, and as the subjective will of man subjects itself to the laws, the antithesis of freedom and necessity disappears. The rational, like the substantial, is necessary. We are free when we recognize it as law and follow it as the substance of our own being. The objective and the subjective will are then reconciled and form one and the same harmonious whole. For the ethos of the state is not of the moral, the reflective kind in which one's own conviction rules supreme. This latter is rather the peculiarity of the modern world. The true and antique morality is rooted in the principle that everybody stands in his place of duty. An Athenian citizen did what was required of him, as it were from instinct. But if I reflect on the object of my activity, I must have the consciousness that my will counts. Morality, however, is the duty, the substantial law, the second nature, as it has been rightly called; for the first nature of man is his immediate, animalic existence.

(b) LAW AS REALIZATION OF FREEDOM

The detailed development of the state is the subject of legal philosophy. But it must be observed that in present-day theories various errors are current respecting the state, which pass for established truths and have become prejudices. We will mention only a few of them, particularly those which refer to the subject of history.

The first error that we encounter is the direct contradiction of our principle that the State is the realization of freedom: the view, namely, that man is free by nature but that in society and in the state, to which he necessarily belongs, he must limit this natural freedom. That man is free "by nature" is quite correct in the sense that he is free according to the very concept of man, that is, in his *destination* only, as he is, in himself; the "nature" of a thing is indeed tantamount to its concept. But the view in question also introduces into the concept of man his immediate and natural way of *existence*. In this sense a state of nature is assumed in which man is imagined in the possession of his natural rights and the unlimited exercise and enjoyment of his freedom. This assumption is not presented as a historical fact; it would indeed be difficult, were the attempt seriously made, to detect any such condition anywhere, either in the present or the past. Primitive conditions can indeed be found, but they are marked by brute passions and acts of violence. Crude as they are, they are at the same time connected with social institutions which, to use the common expression, restrain freedom. The assumption (of the noble savage) is one of those nebulous images which theory produces, an idea which necessarily flows from that theory and to which it ascribes real existence without sufficient historical justification.

Such a state of nature is in theory exactly as we find it in practice. Freedom as the *ideal* of the original state of nature does not *exist* as original and natural. It must first be acquired and won; and that is possible only through an infinite process of the discipline of knowledge and will power. The state of nature, therefore, is rather the state of injustice, violence, untamed natural impulses, of inhuman deeds and emotions. There is, it is true, a limitation by society and the state, but it is a limitation of the brute emotions and rude instincts, as well as (in a more advanced stage of culture) of self-reflecting caprice and passion. This constraint is part of the process through which is first produced the consciousness of and the desire for freedom in its true, that is, rational and ideal form.

The idea of freedom necessarily implies law and morality. These are in and for themselves universal essences, objects, and aims, to be discovered only by the activity of thought, emancipating itself from, and developing itself in opposition to, the merely sensuous; it must be assimilated to and incorporated with the originally sensuous will against its natural inclination. The perpetual misunderstanding of freedom is this: that one knows it only in its formal subjective sense, abstracted from its essential objects and aims. Thus the limitation of impulse, desire, passion—pertaining merely to the particular individual as such—of caprice and willfulness, is taken as a limitation of freedom. On the contrary, such limitation is the very condition leading to liberation; and society and the state are the very conditions in which freedom is realized.

Secondly, there is another theory that objects to the development of morality into legal form. The *patriarchal* state is viewed, either in relation to the whole or to some branches (of the human family), as that condition in which, together with the legal element, the moral and emotional find their fulfillment. Hence justice, it is believed, can be truly carried out only through the union of its content with the moral and emotional elements. The basis of the patriarchal condition is the family relation. It develops as the first phase of conscious morality, to be followed by that of the state as its second phase. The patriarchal condition is one of transition, in which the family has already advanced to a race or people. The union, therefore, has already ceased to be simply a bond of love and confidence and has become one of service. To understand this transition we must first examine the ethical principle of the family. The family is a single person; its members have either, as parents, mutually surrendered their individuality—and consequently their legal relations to one another, as well as their particular interests and desires—or have not yet attained individuality, as children, who are at first in the merely natural condition already mentioned. They live therefore in a unity of feeling, love, confidence, and faith in each other. In love, the one individual has the consciousness of himself in the consciousness of the other; he lives selflessly. In this mutual self-renunciation each gains the life of the other, as well as his own which is one with the other. All other interests of life, its necessities and external concerns, education of the children, form a common purpose for the members of the family. The spirit of the family—the Penates—are as much one substantial being as the spirit of a people in the State. Morality in both cases consists in a feeling, a consciousness, and a will not of the individual personality and its interests but of the common personality, the interest of all members as such. But this unity is in the case of the family essentially one of feeling, remaining within the limits of the natural. The sacredness of the family relation should be respected in the highest degree by the state. Through it the state has as members individuals who are already, as such and in themselves, moral—for as mere persons they are not; and who, in uniting to form a state, bring with them the sound basis of a political edifice, the capacity of feeling one with a whole. But the expansion of the family to a patriarchal whole extends beyond the ties of blood relationship, the simple, natural basis of the state. Beyond that the individuals must acquire the status of personality. A detailed review of the patriarchal condition would lead us to the discussion of theocracy. The head of the patriarchal clan is also its priest. When the family is not yet distinct from civil society and the state, the separation of religion from it has not yet taken place either; and so much the less since its piety is itself (like religion) an inwardness of feeling.

(c) THE LEGAL FOUNDATION OF THE STATE
(THE CONSTITUTION)

We have discussed two aspects of freedom, the objective and the subjective. If freedom implies the consent of each individual, then of course only the subjective aspect is meant. From this principle follows as a matter of course that no law is valid except by agreement of all. This implies that the majority decides; hence the minority must yield to the majority. But already Rousseau has remarked that this means the absence of freedom, for the will of the minority is disregarded. In the Polish diet all decisions had to be unanimous, and it was from this kind of freedom that the state perished. Moreover, it is a dangerous and false presupposition that the people *alone* has reason and insight and knows what is right; for each popular faction can set itself up as the People. What constitutes the state is a matter of trained intelligence, not a matter of "the people."

If the principle of individual will and consent of all is laid down as the only basis of constitutional freedom, then actually there is no *Constitution*. The only institution necessary would be a neutral, centrally located observer who would announce what in his opinion were the needs of the state, a mechanism of assembling the individuals, casting their vote, and the arithmetical counting and comparison of the votes on the various propositions—and this would already be the decision. The state is an abstract entity which has its—merely general—reality in the citizens. But it is real, and the merely general existence must be translated into individual will and activity. Thus arises the necessity of government and administration, the selection of individuals who have to take the helm of political administration, decide its execution, and command the citizens entrusted with it. Thus, even in a democracy the people's decision on a war requires a general as leader of the army. Only in the constitution does the abstract entity of the state assume life and reality; but this involves a distinction between those who command and those who obey. Yet, it does not seem to be in accordance with freedom to obey, and those who command seem to act in opposition to the concept of freedom, the very basis of the state.

Thus the distinction between commanding and obeying seems necessary for the very function of the state. Hence one recommends—as a matter of purely external necessity, which is in opposition to the nature of freedom in its abstract aspect

—that the constitution should at least be so framed that the citizens have to obey as little as possible and the authorities are allowed to command as little as possible. The nature and degree of whatever authority is necessary should be determined and decided in large measure by the people, that is to say, by the will of the majority; yet, at the same time the state, as reality, as individual unit, should have power and strength.

The primary distinction to be made is, then, between the governing and the governed. Constitutions have rightly been classified as monarchic, aristocratic, and democratic; the monarchy proper, however, must be distinguished again from despotism. Also, it must be understood that such classifications are drawn from abstract concepts so as to emphasize the fundamental differences only. They are types or genera or species which cannot exhaustively account for the concrete realities. Particularly, they admit of a great number of special modifications, not only within the types but also among the types; even though such fusions or mixtures of type conduce to misshapen, unstable, and inconsistent forms. The problem, in such collisions, therefore, is to determine the *best constitution,* namely, that institution, organization, or mechanism of government which most securely guarantees the purpose of the state. This goal can of course be considered in various ways, for example, as the quiet enjoyment of life, as universal happiness. Such aims have brought about the so-called ideals of government and, particularly, the ideals of the education of princes, as in Fénelon,[16] or of the rulers or the aristocracy in general, as in Plato. The emphasis is here put on the nature of the ruling individuals; the content of the organic institutions of the state is not at all considered. It is often thought that the question of the best or a better constitution is not

---

[16] In his *Télémaque* (1699), written after Fénelon's tutorship of the Duke of Burgundy, who for a year (1711-1712) was heir-apparent to the throne of Louis XIV. Fénelon (1651-1715) also wrote a *Treatise on the Education of Girls,* which for a century became the standard handbook on the subject. In 1695 he became archbishop of Cambrai. His writings form the transition from absolutism to enlightenment.

only in theory a matter of free individual conviction, but that its actual introduction could also be only a matter of purely theoretical decisions; so that the constitution would be a matter of free choice, determined by nothing but reflection. In this quite naïve sense the Persian magnates—though not the Persian people—deliberated upon the constitution which they wanted to introduce in Persia, after their conspiracy against the pseudo-Smerdis and the Magi had succeeded and there was no royal heir. And the account that Herodotus gives of this deliberation is equally naïve.

Today the constitution of a country and people is not regarded as so entirely dependent upon free choice. The underlying, but abstractly entertained conception of freedom has resulted in the Republic's being quite universally regarded—in theory—as the only just and true constitution. Many of those who even have high official positions under monarchical constitutions do not resist but rather incline toward such views. They understand, however, that such a constitution, though ideal, cannot be realized under all circumstances. People being what they are, one has to be content with less freedom; so that the monarchical constitution, under the given circumstances and the moral condition of the people, is regarded the most useful. Even in this view the actual condition on which the constitution is thought to depend is regarded as a merely external accident. This opinion is based on the separation which reflection and understanding make between the concept and its reality. Holding to an abstract and hence untrue concept they do not grasp the idea; or—which comes to the same thing insofar as the content, though not the form, is concerned—they have no concrete view of a people and a state. We shall show later that the constitution of a people is of the same substance, the same spirit as its art and philosophy, or at least its imagination, its thoughts, and its general culture—not to mention the additional, external influences of climate, neighbors, and global position. A state is an individual totality from which no particular aspect, not even one as highly important as the constitution, can be

separated and considered by itself alone. Nor can this constitution be considered, discussed, and selected in isolation. Not
only is the constitution intimately connected with those other
spiritual forces and dependent on them, but the determination of the whole spiritual individuality, including all its
forces, is only a moment in the history of the whole and predetermined in its course. It is this that gives to the constitution its highest sanction and necessity. The origin of the state
is domination on the one hand, instinctive obedience on the
other. But obedience and force, fear of a ruler, is already a
connection of wills. Already in primitive states we found that
the will of the individual does not count, that particularity
is renounced and the universal will is the essential. This unity
of the universal and the particular is the Idea itself, present as
the State and as such developing itself further. The abstract
but necessary course of the development of truly independent
states begins then with royal power, either patriarchal or military. After that, individuality and particularity must assert
themselves in aristocracy and democracy. The end is the subjection of this particularity under one power which must be
absolutely of such a nature that the two spheres have their
independence outside of it: it must be monarchical. Thus we
must distinguish a first (or original) and a second phase of
royalty. This course is a necessary one; each concrete constitution must enter it. A constitution is therefore not a matter
of choice but depends on the stage of the people's spiritual
development.

What is important in a constitution is the internal development of the rational, that is, the political condition, the setting free of the successive moments of the concept. The particular powers must become distinct, each one completing
itself, but at the same time they must freely cooperate for one
purpose and be held together by it, thus forming an organic
whole. Thus the State is rational and self-conscious freedom,
objectively knowing itself. For its objectivity resides precisely
in the fact that its moments are not merely ideally present but
actualized in their particularity; that they pass over from their

own self-related activity into that activity from which results the whole, the soul, the individual unity.

The State is the idea of Spirit in the externality of human will and its freedom. It therefore is essentially the medium of historical change, and the stages of the Idea represent in it various *principles*. The constitutions wherein world-historical peoples have reached their flowering are peculiar to them, hence give us no universally valid basis. Their differences consist not in the individual manners of elaboration and development, but rather in the differences of principles. Thus we can learn little for the political principle of our time, as the last constitutional principle, from a comparison with the constitutions of earlier world-historical peoples. It is different with science and art. The philosophy of the ancients, for example, is so much the basis of modern philosophy that it must be contained in the latter as its fundament. The relation is here one of uninterrupted development of an identical structure, whose foundations, walls, and roof are still the same. In art that of the Greeks is the highest model. But in respect to the constitution it is different; here the old and the new do not have the essential principle in common, although we do have in common abstract speculations and doctrines of just government, of insight and virtue of the ruler. Yet, nothing is so inappropriate as to use as models for our constitutional institutions examples from Greece, Rome, or the Orient. From the Orient we can take agreeable pictures of patriarchal conditions, fatherly government, popular devotion; from the Greeks and Romans descriptions of popular liberty. The Greeks and Romans understood the concept of a free constitution as granting all citizens a share in the council and decisions of communal affairs and laws. Also in our times this is the general opinion, but with one modification: our states are so big and their people so many, that they cannot directly, but only indirectly through representatives, contribute their will to political decisions. For purposes of legislation the people must be represented by deputies. A free constitution is for us dependent upon the idea of representative government, and this has become a firm prejudice. Thus people and government are separated. But there is something malicious in this opposition, a trick of bad will, as if the people were the whole. Also, at the bottom of this idea lies the principle of individuality, the absoluteness of the subjective will of which we spoke above. The main thing is that freedom, as it is determined by the concept, is *not* based on the subjective will and caprice but on the understanding of the general will, and that the system of freedom is the free development of its stages. The subjective will is a purely formal concept which does not say at all *what* it wills. Only the rational will is the universal which determines and develops itself in itself and unfolds its successive moments in an organic manner. Of such Gothic cathedral architecture the ancients knew nothing.

(d) THE RELIGIOUS FOUNDATION OF THE STATE

We have established as the two points of our discussion, first, the idea of Freedom as absolute final aim, and, secondly, the means of its realization, the subjective side of knowledge and volition with their vitality, mobility, and activity. We then discussed the State as the moral whole and the reality of freedom, and thus as the objective unity of the two preceding factors. Although for analysis we separated the two elements, it must be well remembered that they are closely connected and that this connection is within each of them when we examine them singly. On the one hand we recognized the Idea in its determination, as self-knowing and self-willing freedom which has only itself as its aim. As such, it is at the same time the simple idea of reason and likewise that which we have called subject, the consciousness of self, the Spirit existing in the world. On the other hand, in considering this subjectivity, we find that subjective knowing and willing are Thinking. But in thoughtful knowing and willing I will the universal object, the substance of actualized rationality (of what is in and for itself rational). We thus observe a union which is in itself, between the objective element, the concept,

and the subjective element. The objective existence of this
unity is the State. The State, thus, is the foundation and center of the other concrete aspects of national life, of art, law,
morality, religion, science. All spiritual activity, then, has the
aim of becoming conscious of this union, that is, of its freedom. Among the forms of these conscious unions *religion* is
the highest. In it the spirit existing in the world becomes conscious of absolute Spirit. In this consciousness of actualized
("being-in-and-for-itself") essence the will of man renounces
particular interest; it puts it aside in devotion in which he is
not concerned any more with particulars. Through sacrifice
man expresses his renunciation of property, his will, his private feelings. The religious concentration of the mind appears
as emotion, but passes also into contemplation; ritual is an
expression of contemplation. The second form of the spiritual
union between the objective and the subjective is *Art:* it appears more in sensible reality than does religion; in its most
noble attitude it has to represent, not indeed the spirit of God
but the form of the God—and then the divine, the spiritual in
general. It renders the divine visible to imagination and the
senses. The True, however, not only achieves representation
and feeling, as in religion, and for the senses, as in art, but
also for the thinking spirit; this leads to the third form of the
union, *Philosophy.* It is in this respect the highest, freest, and
wisest product. We cannot here discuss these three forms in
any detail. They had to be mentioned only because they
occupy the same ground as the object of our study, the *State.*

The universal which appears and becomes known in the
state, the form into which is cast all reality, constitutes what
is generally called the *culture* of a nation.[17] The definite
content, however, which receives the form of universality and
is contained in the concrete reality of the State, is the *spirit
of the people.* The true State is animated by this spirit in all
its affairs, wars, institutions, etc. But man must himself know
of this—his own—spirit and essence and give himself the consciousness of his original union with it. For we said that all

[17] See above, p. 52.

morality is the unity of subjective and general will. The spirit, then, must give itself an express consciousness of this unity, and the center of this knowledge is religion. Art and science are only different aspects of this very same content.

In discussing religion it is important to ask whether it recognizes truth, or the Idea, only in its separation or in its true unity. In its separation: when God is conceived as the abstract highest Being, Lord of Heaven and Earth, transcending the world, beyond, and excluded from, human reality—or in its unity: God as unity of the universal and particular, in Whom even the particular is positively regarded, in the idea of incarnation. Religion is the sphere where a people gives itself the definition of what it regards as the True. Such a definition contains everything which belongs to the essence of the object, reducing its nature to a simple fundamental characteristic as focus for all other characteristics—the universal soul of all particulars. The idea of God thus is the general fundament of a people.

In this respect religion stands in closest connection with the principle of the State. Freedom can only exist where individuality is known as positive in the divine Being. There is a further connection between religion and the state: secular existence is temporal and moves within private interest. Hence it is relative and unjustified. Its justification can only be derived from the absolute justification of its universal soul, its principle. And this is justified only as determination and existence of the essence of God. For this reason the State is based on religion. We hear this often repeated in our time. But mostly nothing more is meant than that individuals should be pious in order to be more willing and prepared to do their duty; for obedience to prince and law is so easily connected with reverence toward God. It is true that reverence toward God, in elevating the universal over the particular, can turn against the particular in fanaticism, and work against the State, burning and destroying its buildings and institutions. Hence reverence for God, it is believed, should be temperate and kept in a certain degree of coolness, lest it storm

against and destroy that which ought to be protected and preserved by it. The possibility of such disaster is at least latent
in it.

The correct conviction that the State rests on religion may
give religion a position which presupposes the existence of
the State. Then, in order to preserve the State, religion must
be carried into it, in buckets and bushels, in order to impress
it upon people's minds. It is quite correct that man must be
educated to religion, but not as to something which does not
yet exist. For, when we say that the State is based on religion
and that it has its roots in it, we mean essentially that it has
arisen from it and now and always continues to arise out
of it. That is, the principles of the State must be regarded as
valid in and for themselves, which they can only insofar as
they are known to be determinations of divine nature itself.
The nature of its religion, therefore, determines that of the
State and its constitution. It actually has originated from it:
the Athenian and the Roman states were possible only
through the specific paganism of these peoples, just as a
Catholic state has a spirit and constitution different from
a Protestant one.

It would be bad if this appeal, this urge and drive to implant religion, were a call of anguish and distress, as it looks so
often—as if it expressed the danger that religion were about to
disappear or already had disappeared from the State. Indeed,
it would be worse than this appeal assumes; for it assumes
it can still implant and inculcate religion as a means against
this evil. But religion is not such an artifact. Its self-produc-
tion is a much more profound process. Another and opposite
folly which we meet in our time is the tendency to invent and
institute constitutions independently from religion. The Catholic religion, although, like the Protestant, part of Christianity,
does not concede to the State the inner justice and morality
which follows from the inwardness of the Protestant principle.
This separation of constitutional law and of constitutions
themselves from morality is necessary because of the peculiarity of that religion; it does not regard law and morality as

independent and substantial. But thus torn away from inwardness, from the last sanctuary of conscience, from the quiet
corner where religion has its abode, the constitutional principles and institutions lack a real center and remain abstract
and indeterminate.

In summary, the vitality of the State in individuals is what
we call Morality.[18] The State, its laws, its institutions are the
rights of the citizens; its nature, its soil, its mountains, air,
and waters are their land, their country, their external property. The history of the State are their deeds, and what their
ancestors have accomplished belongs to them and lives in
their memory. Everything is their possession just as they are
possessed by it, for it constitutes their substance and being.

Their minds are full of it and their wills are their willing
of these laws and of their country. It is this temporal totality
which is One Being, the spirit of One People. To it the individuals belong; each individual is the son of his people and,
at the same time, insofar as his state is in development, the
son of his age. No one remains behind it, no one can leap
ahead of it. This spiritual being is his—he is one of its representatives—it is that from which he arises and wherein he
stands. For the Athenians Athens had a double meaning, the
totality of their institutions as well as the goddess which represented the spirit and the unity of the people.

This spirit of a people is a *definite* spirit and, as was just
said, is also determined according to the historical state of
its development. This spirit, then, is the basis and content
of the other forms of consciousness which have been mentioned. For the spirit in its consciousness of itself must be
concrete to itself. Its objectivity immediately contains the
origin of differences, which in their totality are the various
spheres of the objective spirit itself—just as the soul exists
only as the organization of its members which constitute it by
combining themselves into simple unity. Thus it is one individuality. Its essence is represented, revered, and enjoyed as

---

[18] Objective *Sittlichkeit* fused with subjective *Moralität*. See Introduction, p. xxxii.

God, in religion; presented as image and intuition, in art; apprehended cognitively and conceived as thought, in philosophy. Because of the original identity of their substance, their content, and their subject matter with that of the State these products are inseparably united with the spirit of the State. Only with such a religion can there be such a form of the State, and only with such a State such art and such philosophy.

Furthermore, the definite national spirit itself is only one individual in the course of world history. For world history is the manifestation of the Divine, the absolute process of Spirit in its highest forms. It is this development wherein it achieves its truth and the consciousness of itself. The products of its stages are the world-historical national spirits, the definiteness of their moral life, their constitution, art, religion, and science. To realize these stages is the infinite élan of the World Spirit, its irresistible urge; for this differentiation and its realization constitute its concept. World history only shows how the World Spirit gradually attains the consciousness and willing of truth. Dawn rises in the Spirit; it discovers focal points; [19] and finally, it attains full consciousness.

[19] Cf. the account of the Spirit's epistemological self-differentiation, from the form of gesture up to that of modern science, in Ernst Cassirer's *Philosophie der symbolischen Formen, Berlin,* 1923-1929. English trans. by Ralph Manheim, *The Philosophy of Symbolic Forms* (New Haven, Yale U. Press, 1953).

IV. THE COURSE OF WORLD HISTORY

1. THE PRINCIPLE OF DEVELOPMENT

We have now learned the abstract characteristics of the nature of Spirit, the means which it uses to realize its Idea, and the form which its complete realization assumes in external existence, namely, the State. All that remains for this introduction is to consider the *course of world history*.

Historical change, seen abstractly, has long been understood generally as involving a progress toward the better, the more perfect. Change in nature, no matter how infinitely varied it is, shows only a cycle of constant repetition. In nature nothing new happens under the sun, and in this respect the multiform play of her products leads to boredom. One and the same permanent character continuously reappears, and all change reverts to it. Only the changes in the realm of Spirit create the novel. This characteristic of Spirit suggested to man a feature entirely different from that of nature—the desire toward *perfectibility*. This principle, which brings change itself under laws, has been badly received by religions such as the Catholic and also by states which desire as their true right to be static or at least stable. When the mutability of secular things, such as states, is conceded on principle, then religion, as religion of truth, is excluded. On the other hand, one leaves undecided whether changes, revolutions, and destructions of legitimate conditions are not due to accidents, blunders, and, in particular, the license and evil passions of men. Actually, perfectibility is something almost as undetermined as mutability in general; it is without aim and purpose and without a standard of change. The better, the more perfect toward which it is supposed to attain, is entirely undetermined.

The principle of *development* implies further that it is based on an inner principle, a presupposed potentiality, which

68

brings itself into existence. This formal determination is essentially the Spirit whose scene, property, and sphere of realization is world history. It does not flounder about in the external play of accidents. On the contrary, it is absolutely determined and firm against them. It uses them for its own purposes and dominates them. But development is also a property of organic natural objects. Their existence is not merely dependent, subject to external influences. It proceeds from an inner immutable principle, a simple essence, which first exists as germ. From this simple existence it brings forth out of itself differentiations which connect it with other things. Thus it lives a life of continuous transformation. On the other hand, we may look at it from the opposite point of view and see in it the preservation of the organic principle and its form. Thus the organic individual produces itself; it makes itself actually into that which it is in itself (potentially). In the same way, Spirit is only that into which it makes itself, and it makes itself actually into that which it is in itself (potentially). The development of the organism proceeds in an immediate, direct (undialectic), unhindered manner. Nothing can interfere between the concept and its realization, the inherent nature of the germ and the adaptation of its existence to this nature. It is different with Spirit. The transition of its potentiality into actuality is mediated through consciousness and will. These are themselves first immersed in their immediate organic life; their first object and purpose is this natural existence as such. But the latter, through its animation by Spirit, becomes itself infinitely demanding, rich, and strong. Thus Spirit is at war with itself. It must overcome itself as its own enemy and formidable obstacle. Development, which in nature is a quiet unfolding, is in Spirit a hard, infinite struggle against itself. What Spirit wants is to attain its own concept. But it hides it from itself and is proud and full of enjoyment in this alienation from itself.

Historical development, therefore, is not the harmless and unopposed simple growth of organic life but hard, unwilling labor against itself. Furthermore, it is not mere formal self-development in general, but the production of an end of determined content. This end we have stated from the beginning: it is Spirit in its essence, the concept of freedom. This is the fundamental object and hence the leading principle of development. Through it the development receives meaning and significance—just as in Roman history Rome is the object and hence the guiding principle of the inquiry into past events. At the same time, however, the events arise out of this object and have meaning and content only with reference to it.

There are in world history several large periods which have passed away, apparently without further development. Their whole enormous gain of culture has been annihilated and, unfortunately, one had to start all over from the beginning in order to reach again one of the levels of culture which had been reached long ago—assisted, perhaps, by some ruins saved of old treasures—with a new, immeasurable effort of power and time, of crime and suffering. On the other hand, there are continuing developments, structures, and systems of culture in particular spheres, rich in kind and well-developed in every direction. The merely formal view of development can give preference neither to one course nor the other; nor can it account for the purpose of that decline of older periods. It must consider such events, and in particular such reversals, as external accidents. It can judge the relative advantages only according to indefinite viewpoints—viewpoints which are relative precisely because development *in general* is viewed as the one and only purpose.

World history, then, represents the phases in the development of the principle whose *content* is the consciousness of freedom. The analysis of its stages in general belongs to Logic. That of its particular, its concrete nature, belongs to the Philosophy of Spirit.[1] Let us only repeat here that the first stage is the immersion of Spirit in natural life, the second its stepping out into the consciousness of its freedom. This first

[1] The *Phänomenologie des Geistes*, 1807. English translation by Baillie, 1910, 1931.

emancipation from nature is incomplete and partial; it issues from immediate naturalness, still refers to it, and hence is still incumbered by it as one of its elements. The third stage is the rising out of this still particular form of freedom into pure universality of freedom, where the spiritual essence attains the consciousness and feeling of itself. These stages are the fundamental principles of the universal process. Each is again, within itself, a process of its own formation. But the detail of this inner dialectic of transition must be left to the sequel.

All we have to indicate here is that Spirit begins with its infinite possibility, but *only* its possibility. As such it contains its absolute content within itself, as its aim and goal, which it attains only as result of its activity. Then and only then has Spirit attained its reality. Thus, in existence, progress appears as an advance from the imperfect to the more perfect. But the former must not only be taken in abstraction as the merely imperfect, but as that which contains at the same time its own opposite, the so-called perfect, as germ, as urge within itself. In the same way, at least in thought, possibility points to something which shall become real; more precisely, the Aristotelian *dynamis* is also *potentia*, force and power. The imperfect, thus, as the opposite of itself in itself, is its own antithesis, which on the one hand exists, but, on the other, is annulled and resolved. It is the urge, the impulse of spiritual life in itself, to break through the hull of nature, of sensuousness, of its own self-alienation, and to attain the light of consciousness, namely, its own self.

2. THE ORIGIN OF HISTORY

(a) THE PRE-HISTORY OF REASON

We have already discussed how the beginning of the history of Spirit must be understood in terms of the concept of freedom, when we referred to the "state of nature" in which freedom and justice would be, or have been, perfectly actualized.

This however was only an assumption, the assumption of an historical existence presented in the twilight of hypothesis. There is another assumption of an entirely different kind put into circulation today by certain parties, a pretension which is not presented as a theoretical hypothesis, but as an historical fact; and not only as an historical fact, but as a fact verified by higher sanction. This pretension takes up again the old notion of a primary, paradisical state of man, which the theologians had elaborated after their fashion by asserting, for example, that God had spoken with Adam in Hebrew. This is today revised in accordance with other interests. The higher authority in question is the Biblical account. But this account, on the one hand, represents the primitive conditions only through the few traits that are known. On the other hand, it either considers these traits as belonging to man in general, that is, to human nature as such; or it regards Adam as a particular individual and thus considers these primitive traits as belonging to one human person or to one human couple only. Yet these interpretations do not justify the opinion that a people has existed historically in such primitive conditions, and still less, that the pure knowledge of God and nature has been formed therein. Nature, so the fiction runs,[2] originally stood open and transparent before the clear eye of man, as a bright mirror of divine creation, and the divine truth was equally open to him. It is even hinted—yet at the same time left in some degree of obscurity—that in this primary condition men had been in possession of an indefinite, already quite extensive knowledge of religious truths immediately revealed by God. From this supposedly historical condition, then, all religions are said to have taken their origin. But in the process, the original truth had been polluted and obscured by monstrous errors and perversions. Yet in all the mythologies invented by such error, traces of that origin and those first religious truths are supposed to be present and recognized. Investigations of the history of ancient peoples are therefore essentially interested

[2] Fr. v. Schlegel, *Philosophy of History,* "Bohn's Standard Library," p. 91.

in going back to a point where such fragments of first revealed insight are still to be found in greater purity.[3]

We owe to this interest a great deal of valuable investigations. But this investigation immediately testifies against itself because it tends to verify as historical only that which it has presupposed as historical. Thus, world history is said to have had its origin in this knowledge of God or in scientific notions, such as astronomical knowledge allegedly possessed by the Hindus. From such beginnings, it is then held, the religions of the peoples had taken their traditional point of departure, but subsequently they had been perverted and de-

[3] We have to thank this interest for many valuable discoveries in Oriental literature and for a renewed study of treasures previously recorded regarding ancient Asiatic culture, mythology, religions, and history. In Catholic countries, where a refined literary taste prevails, Governments have yielded to the requirements of speculative inquiry, and have felt the necessity of allying themselves with learning and philosophy. Eloquently and impressively the Abbé Lamennais has reckoned it among the criteria of the true religion that it must be the universal—that is, Catholic—and the oldest in date; and the Congregation has labored zealously and diligently in France towards rendering such assertions no longer mere pulpit tirades and authoritative dicta, such as were deemed sufficient formerly. The religion of Buddha—a god-man—which has prevailed to such an enormous extent, has especially attracted attention. The Indian Timurtis, like the Chinese abstraction of the Trinity, has furnished clearer evidence in point of subject matter. The scholars, M. Abel Remusat and M. Saint Martin, on the one hand, have undertaken the most meritorious investigations in the Chinese literature with a view to making this also a base of operations for researches in the Mongolian and, if possible, the Tibetan. On the other hand, Baron von Eckstein, after his fashion (i.e., adopting from Germany superficial conceptions of natural philosophy and mannerisms in the style of Fr. v. Schlegel, though with more geniality than the latter) in his periodical, *Le Catholique*—has furthered the cause of that primitive Catholicism generally, and in particular has gained for the scholars of the Congregation the support of the government. As a consequence, expeditions have even been sent to the East in order to discover there treasures still concealed (from which further disclosures have been anticipated, respecting profound theological questions, particularly on the higher antiquity and sources of Buddhism), and with a view to promoting the interests of Catholicism by this circuitous but scientifically interesting method.—*Author*

generated, for example, in the crudely conceived so-called systems of emanation. All these are subjective, arbitrary assump-
tions, which neither have nor can have any historical justification in the light of the true conception of history.

Philosophical investigation can and ought to take up the
study of history only where Reason begins to assume worldly
existence, where consciousness, will, and action appear, and
not where all this is still an unrealized possibility. The un-
organic existence of Spirit, the still unconscious dullness—or,
if you will, excellence—of freedom, of good and evil and
thereby of laws, is not the object of history. The natural and
at the same time religious morality is the piety of the *family*.
Morality in this society consists in the very fact that its members behave toward each other not out of free will as individuals, not as persons. It is for this very reason that the
family is still excluded from the development in which history
takes its rise (it is pre-historical). Only when spiritual unity
steps beyond this circle of feeling and natural love, and arrives at the consciousness of personality, does that obscure
and rigid nucleus emerge in which neither nature nor spirit
are open and transparent and where both can become open
and transparent only through the further working of that self-
conscious will and, indeed, through the long drawn-out cultural process, the goal of which is very remote. For consciousness alone is that which is open, that to which God and anything else can reveal itself. Nothing can reveal itself in its
truth, in its concrete universality (for itself), unless there is a
consciousness aware of itself. Freedom is nothing but the
recognition and adoption of such universal substantial objects
as Right and Law and the production of a reality which is in
accordance with them—the State.

Peoples may have continued a long life before they reach
their destination of becoming a state. They may even have
attained considerable culture in certain directions. This *pre-
history*, according to what has been said, lies outside of our
plan. Subsequently, these peoples may either have had a real
history or never attained the formation of a state. During the

last twenty-odd years a great discovery, as if of a new world, has been made in history, that of the Sanskrit language and its connection with the European languages. This has given us an insight into the connection of the Germanic and Indian peoples, a theory which carries as much certainty as such matters allow. Thus, at present we know quite certainly that there existed peoples which scarcely formed a society, let alone a state, but which nevertheless are known to have existed for a long time. Of others whose civilized condition interests us greatly the tradition reaches back beyond the history of the origin of their state. Much has happened to them before. This linguistic connection of so widely separated peoples shows as an irrefutable fact the spread of these peoples from Asia as a center and, at the same time, the disparate differentiation of an original kinship. This fact, fortunately, does not arise from the favorite method of combining and embellishing all kinds of circumstances, which has enriched and continues to enrich history with so many fictions presented as facts. Yet, this apparently so extensive range of events lies outside of history; it preceded it.

(b) THE STATE AS CONDITION OF HISTORY

History combines in our language the objective as well as the subjective side. It means both the *historiam rerum gestarum* and the *res gestas* themselves, both the events and the narration of the events. (It means both *Geschehen* and *Geschichte*.) This connection of the two meanings must be regarded as highly significant and not merely accidental. We must hold that the narration of history and historical deeds and events appear at the same time; a common inner principle brings them forth together. Family memories, patriarchal traditions have an interest confined to the family and the tribe. The uniform course of events under such conditions is not an object for memory. But distinctive events or turns of fortune may rouse Mnemosyne to form images of them, just as love and religious sentiments stimulate the imagination to give shape to an originally formless impulse. But it is the State which first presents subject matter that is not only appropriate for the prose of history but creates it together with itself. A community which acquires a stable existence and elevates itself into a state requires more than merely subjective mandates of government, sufficient only for the needs of the moment. It requires rules, laws, universal and universally valid norms. It thus produces a record of, and interest in, intelligent, definite, and in their effects lasting actions and events. To these, Mnemosyne, in order to perpetuate the formation and constitution of the State, is impelled to add duration by remembrance. Deeper sensitivity in general, like that of love and religious insight and its images, are in themselves complete, constantly present, and satisfying. But the state has (not only an internal but)—in rational laws and customs—at the same time an external existence. Thus its mere present state is incomplete; its complete understanding requires the consciousness of the past.

The periods, whether we suppose them to be centuries or millennia, which peoples have passed before the writing of history, may have been filled with revolutions, migrations, the wildest transformations. Yet, they are without objective history because they lack subjective history, records of history. Such records are lacking, not because they have accidentally disappeared during those long ages, but because they never could have existed.

Only in the state with the consciousness of laws are there clear actions, and is the consciousness of them clear enough to make the keeping of records possible and desired. It is striking to everyone who becomes acquainted with the treasures of Indian literature that that country, so rich in spiritual products of greatest profundity, has no history. In this it contrasts strikingly with China, which possesses such an excellent history going back to the oldest times. India not only has old books of religion and brilliant works of poetry but also old codes of law—which above were mentioned as a condition of the formation of history—and yet it has no history. In that country the impulse of organization, which begins to differentiate society, was immediately petrified into the natural distinctions of castes. The laws, thus, concern the civil rights, but make them dependent on these natural distinctions. They determine primarily mutual *prerogatives* of the castes—wrongs rather than rights—namely, of the higher against the lower. Therewith the element of morality is banished from the splendor of Indian life and its empires. Because of that bondage of the caste system, in all historical relation there is wild arbitrariness, ephemeral bustling, indeed, raging without a final purpose of progress or development. Thus there is no thinking memory, no object present for Mnemosyne. A deep yet wild fantasy roams all over the ground; whereas, to create history, it would have needed a purpose within reality, belonging at the same time to substantial freedom.

(c) THE HISTORICAL ROLE OF LANGUAGE

Due to such a condition of history this rich, indeed immeasurable growth of families into tribes, of tribes into nations, and their expansion due to this increase—a series of events which itself suggests so many complications, wars, rebellions, ruins—all this has merely happened without real history. What is more, the extension and organic growth of the realm of sounds connected with this process itself remained voiceless and dumb—a stealthy unnoticed advance. It is a fact of philological evidence that the languages that peoples have spoken in their rude conditions were highly elaborate; the understanding threw itself with great ingenuity and completeness into this theoretical task. A comprehensive, consistent grammar is the work of thought which reveals its categories in it. It is, moreover, a fact that with advancing social and political civilization this systematic product of intelligence is blunted, and language becomes poorer and less subtle. It is a strange phenomenon that the progress toward greater spiritualization and emphasized rationality should neglect this intelligent prolixity and expressiveness and actually find it cumbersome and dispensable.[4] Language is the work of theoretical intelligence in the true sense; it is its external expression. Without language the exercises of memory and fantasy are immediate (non-speculative) manifestations. But this theoretical achievement in general and its further development, as well as the concrete fact connected with it—the spreading of peoples over the earth, their separations from one another, their comminglings and wanderings—all this remains veiled in the obscurity of a voiceless past. These are not acts of a will becoming conscious of itself, not acts of freedom giving itself phenomenal form and true reality. These peoples do not partake of the true element of history, in spite of their development of language. Therefore they have not attained historical existence. The premature growth of language and the progress and dispersion of nations gains significance and interest for concrete Reason only in either the contact with states or the autonomous formation of states.

3. THE COURSE OF DEVELOPMENT

So much for the beginning of world history and the prehistorical periods to be excluded from it. We must now more closely examine the manner of its course, though here only formally. The concrete content will be dealt with in the main part.

(a) THE PRINCIPLE OF A PEOPLE

World history, as already shown, represents the development of the Spirit's consciousness of freedom and the consequent realization of that freedom. This development implies a gradual progress, a series of ever more concrete differentiations, as involved in the concept of freedom. The logical and,

---

[4] This is not so strange as Hegel thinks. The process from elaborateness to simplicity of language is a process from concreteness to abstraction. While the language becomes poorer in concrete expressions (e.g. the 5744 words for "camel" in nomadic Arabic) it becomes richer in symbolic reference.

even more, the dialectical nature of the concept in general, the necessity of its purely abstract self-development, is treated in Logic. There it is shown that it determines itself, posits its own determinations and in turn abolishes them (transcending itself), and by this very process of abolition and transcending gains an affirmative, ever richer and more concretely determined form. Here we have to adopt only one of its results: that each stage, being different from the other, has its definite, peculiar principle. Such a principle is in history the differentiation of Spirit; it is a particular national spirit. In this particular form a national spirit expresses concretely all the aspects of its will and consciousness, its whole reality. This principle defines the common features of its religion, its political constitution, its morality, its system of law, its mores, even its science, art, and technical skill. These special particularities must be understood in the light of the universal particularity,[5] the special principle of a people. Conversely, that universal may be detected in the historically present factual detail of the particulars.

That the particular principle of a people is indeed a definite particularity is a point which must be empirically examined and historically proved. This presupposes not only a practiced faculty of abstraction, but also an intimate acquaintance with the Idea. One has to be familiar, so to speak, a priori, with the whole sphere of conceptions to which the principles belong, just as Kepler, to mention the greatest man in this mode of thinking, must have been acquainted a priori with ellipses, cubes, and squares and their relations. Only thus, by application of these mathematical concepts to the empirical data, was he able to invent his immortal laws, which consist in determinations of those concepts.[6] He who is ignorant of the science embracing these elementary definitions

[5] The "principle" is universal with respect to the cultural forms but particular with respect to Spirit.

[6] In other words, just as one must know mathematics before applying it to nature so one must know the dialectic of the Idea before applying it to history.

can neither understand nor invent those laws, no matter how long he looks at the sky and the motions of the stars. This unfamiliarity with the Idea of the self-development of Freedom gives rise to some of the reproaches which are leveled against the philosophical treatment of a supposedly empirical science, in particular against the so-called a priori method and the introduction of ideas into the empirical data of history. Such ideas then appear as something foreign to the material. To a mind which lacks both knowledge and discipline of thought they certainly are foreign and beyond the conception which its ignorance forms of the object. Hence the statement that philosophy does not understand such sciences. Philosophy must indeed concede that it does not have the kind of understanding which rules in these sciences and does not proceed according to the categories of such understanding. Rather, it follows the categories of Reason. But these enable it to know not only this understanding but also its value and systematic position. It is equally necessary in this procedure of scientific understanding to separate the essential from the unessential and to bring both into relief against each other. To do so, however, one must know the essential; and the essential in world history, seen as a whole, is the consciousness of freedom and the realization of that consciousness in developing itself. The direction toward this category is the direction toward the truly essential.

Part of the arguments and objections raised against such a determination through universals arises usually through the lack of comprehension and understanding of ideas. If in natural history a monstrous or hybrid growth is brought forward as example against the tidy order of species and classes, then one can rightly apply what is often said vaguely, that the exception proves the rule—which is to say that it is up to the rule to demonstrate the condition under which it applies and to show up the deficiency, the hybridism, which lies in the deviation from the normal. Mere nature is too weak to keep its genera and species pure against conflicting elemental influences. If, e.g., on considering the human organization in its concrete aspect, we assert that brain, heart, and so forth are essential to its organic life, some miserable abortion may be adduced which has on the whole the human form or parts of it. It has been generated in a human body, has lived in it, and has breathed after birth, yet no brain and no heart is found in it. If such an instance is quoted against the general concept of a human being—the objector persisting in using the name coupled with a superficial idea of it—it can be proved that a real concrete human being is a truly different object. It must have a brain in its head, and a heart in its breast.

A similar mode of reasoning is used when it is rightly said that genius, talents, piety, moral virtues and sentiments appear in all zones, under all constitutions, and political conditions. There is an abundance of examples to confirm this. However, if such an assertion means to repudiate these distinctions as unimportant or unessential, then thinking stops at abstract categories and disregards any specific content—for which, it is true, no principle can be supplied by these categories. The viewpoint that adopts such merely formal perspectives presents a vast field for ingenious questions, erudite views, and striking comparisons, seemingly profound reflections and declamations, which can be the more brilliant, the more indefinite their subject is. Moreover, they can be renewed and varied again and again in inverse proportion to the certainty and rationality to be gained by their efforts. In this sense the well-known Indian epics can be compared with the Homeric and, taking vastness of imagination as proof of poetical genius, can be put above them. Or, one may find similarity in some fantastic features of Greek and Indian divinities and claim to recognize figures of Greek mythology in those of India. Again, the *One (Tao)* in Chinese philosophy has been held to be the same as that which at later periods appeared in Eleatic philosophy $\tau\grave{o}\ \accentset{\backprime}{\epsilon}\nu\ \kappa\alpha\grave{\iota}\ \pi\hat{\alpha}\nu$ and in the Spinozistic system *(Substance)*. Also, because it expresses itself in abstract numbers and lines, one has seen in it Pythagorean and Christian features. Instances of courage, persisting fortitude, features of nobility, of self-denial and self-sacrifice, which are found among the most savage and the most pusillanimous nations, are regarded as sufficient proof that there is as much or even more morality and ethics in them as in the most civilized Christian states, and so on. On this ground, then, the doubt has been raised whether men in the progress of history and the development of culture have become better at all, whether their morality has increased—morality here being understood only as the subjective intention and insight of the agent, his own view of what is right or wrong, good or bad, and not as a principle which in and for itself is right and good, bad and evil, nor as a particular religion believed to be the true one.

We do not have to make evident the formalism and error of such a view, nor to establish the true principles of morality —or rather, establish ethics against false morality. For the history of the world moves on a higher level than that proper to morality. The locus of morality is private sentiment, individual conscience, particular will and mode of action. These have their own appropriate value, responsibility, reward, or punishment. The demands and accomplishments of the absolute and final aim of Spirit, the working of Providence, lie above the obligations, responsibilities, and liabilities which are incumbent on the individuals in regard to their morality. (An individual may for moral reasons resist and for immoral reasons advance the course of history.) Those who through moral steadfastness and noble sentiment have resisted the necessary progress of the Spirit stand higher in moral value than those whose crimes have been turned by a higher purpose into means of carrying on the will behind this purpose. But in revolutions of this kind both parties stand within the same circle of disaster. It is therefore only a formal right, forsaken both by the living spirit and by God, which the defenders of ancient right and order (no matter how moral) maintain. The deeds of the great men who are the individuals of world history thus appear justified not only in their intrinsic, unconscious significance but also from the point of view of world history. It is irrelevant and inappropriate from that point of view to raise moral claims against world-historical acts and agents. They stand outside of morality. The litany of the private virtues of modesty, humility, love, and charity must not be raised against them. World history (if it wanted to) could on principle altogether ignore the sphere of morality and its often mentioned difference with politics. It could not only refrain from moral judgments—its principles and the necessary relations of actions to them already are the judgment—but leave individuals entirely out of view and unmentioned. For what it has to record are the actions of the spirits of peoples. The individual forms which that spirit assumes in the sphere of external reality could be left to historiography in the narrow sense.

The same formalism which finds everything everywhere also plays around with vague ideas of genius, poetry, and philosophy, and finds them, too, everywhere alike. These ideas are products of a purely general reflection, which singles out and names essential distinctions, moving around with agility without going to the bottom of the matter. In this way we get *general culture*—something merely formal which aims at nothing more than the analysis of a subject, whatever it may be, into its constituent elements and the comprehension of these elements through conceptual definitions and forms of thought. This is not the free universality which has to be made for itself an object of consciousness. Such consciousness of thought itself and of its forms isolated from all content is philosophy. The condition of its existence is indeed general culture, for its function is to invest the given content with the form of universality. Thus its possession involves both content and form in inseparable connection, so inseparable, indeed, that the content is regarded as purely empirical, without any admixture of thought. In this way analysis of an idea into a multitude of ideas enlarges the content itself to immeasurable richness. But it is quite as much an act of *thought*, namely of the understanding, to make an object which in itself comprehends a rich concrete content into a simple idea and designate it by one name [7]—such as, *Earth, Man,* or *Alexander* and *Caesar*—as it is to analyze the Idea, isolate in thought the meanings it contains, and give them particular names. From all this follows that just as reflection brings forth the universal concepts of *Genius, Talent, Art, Science,* so formal culture on every stage of intellectual development not only can but must prosper and reach a high bloom when it (reaches abstract, universal reflection. This it does when it) forms itself into a state. For on such a foundation civilization progresses to reflective understanding and abstract universality, not only in laws but in everything. In the life of the State as such lies the necessity of formal culture and therewith of the rise of sciences and of a finer poetry and art in general. Besides, the fine arts require even on the technical side the civilized association of men. Poetry is less in need of external necessities and tools and has as its material an element of immediate (natural) existence in the human voice. Hence it emerges with great vitality and fully developed already at a stage when a people has not yet attained unity through law. For, as was remarked earlier, language reaches a high development of thought before the beginning of civilization.

Philosophy, too, must make its appearance in the life of a state. For that process whereby a content becomes an element of culture is, as has just been shown, the form belonging to thought. Thus, philosophy, which is but the consciousness of that form itself, the thinking of thinking, receives the proper material for her own building already prepared from general culture. In the development of the State itself, periods must occur which impel the spirit of nobler natures to escape from the present into ideal regions, where they may find the reconciliation with themselves, which in the disintegrated real world they can no longer enjoy. During such periods the reflecting understanding attacks everything holy and deep which has been naïvely introduced into religion, laws, and customs. It flattens and dissipates it into abstract, godless gen-

[7] This is the function Hegel failed to connect with the development of language. See note 4, p. 78.

eralities. Thus thinking is compelled to become thinking Reason in order to attempt in its own element the restoration from the ruin to which thought has been brought.

To be sure, we then find poetry, fine arts, science, and even philosophy in all world-historical peoples. But not only are style and direction different in general, but the content is even more different. And this content concerns the highest difference, that of rationality. (It is wrong to say that it is form, not content, that counts.) It is of no help when pretentious aesthetic criticism demands that the material, the substantial of the content, ought not to determine our aesthetic pleasure, but that beautiful form as such, or greatness of imagination and the like, is the aim of the arts; it is claimed that it is this which ought to be noticed and enjoyed by a liberal taste and cultivated mind. Sound common sense does not tolerate such abstractions and does not assimilate works of that kind. Granted that the Hindu epics might be placed side by side with the Homeric because of a great number of such formal properties—greatness of invention and imagination, liveliness of images and emotions, beauty of diction—there still remains the infinite difference of content, and hence the essential. There remains the interest of Reason which aims directly at the consciousness of the concept of freedom and its development in individuals. There is not only a classical form but also a classical subject-matter. Furthermore, content and form are so closely combined in a work of art that the former can be classical only as far as the latter is. With a fantastic content which does not limit itself intrinsically—and the reasonable is precisely that which has measure and purpose in itself—the form itself loses measure and form, or else (by contrast with the content) becomes petty and painfully narrow. In the comparison of the various philosophies, which we mentioned earlier, only one point of importance is being overlooked, namely, the *nature* of that unity which is found alike in Chinese, Eleatic, and Spinozistic philosophy. Is this unity grasped as abstract or concrete and, if concrete, does this concreteness go to the point of being a unity in and for itself, a unity synonymous with Spirit? [8] This equalization, however, proves that one recognizes a merely abstract unity. Thus, in judging about philosophy, one ignores that which constitutes the very interest of philosophy.

There are, however, also spheres which despite all the variety of cultural contents remain the same. This variety of cultures concerns thinking Reason, freedom whose self-consciousness Reason is and which springs from the same root as Thought. As it is not the animal but man alone who thinks, so also he alone has freedom—and only because he thinks. His consciousness makes the individual comprehend himself as a person, in his uniqueness as a universal in himself, capable of abstraction, of surrendering all particularity, hence understanding himself as inherently infinite. Spheres, therefore, that lie outside of this understanding (that is, are not individual) are common ground for these cultural differences. Even morals, which are so intimately connected with the consciousness of freedom, can be very pure even though this consciousness be still lacking. They then express only the general duties and rights as objective commandments, or stop at merely negative norms, such as the formal elevation of the soul, the surrender of sensuality and of all sensual motives. *Chinese* morals gained highest praise and recognition from the Europeans as soon as this ethics and the writings of Confucius became known to them, and particularly by those who were familiar with Christian morals. Also the sublimity is recognized with which *Indian* religion, philosophy, and poetry—that is, its higher form—express and demand the elimination and sacrifice of sensuality. However, these two nations, it must be said, lack completely the essential consciousness of the concept of freedom. To the Chinese their moral laws are like laws of nature—external, positive commands, compulsory rights and duties, or rules of politeness toward one another. The freedom is lacking through which alone the substantial determinations of Reason become moral con-

[8] First edition: ". . . is this concreteness that of greatest concreteness, that of Spirit."

viction. Morals are a matter of the state and handled by officials of the government and the courts.[9] Their treatises about it, which are not legal codes but addressed to the subjective will and disposition, read like the moral writings of the Stoics—a series of norms which are supposed to be necessary for the purpose of happiness; so that it is apparently up to the individual to take his stand toward them: he may or may not obey them. Indeed, it is the representation of an abstract subject, the sage, which for the Chinese as for the Stoic moralists is the culmination of such doctrines. Also in the Indian doctrine of renunciation of sensuality, of desires, and worldly interests, the aim and purpose are not affirmative moral freedom, but the annihilation of consciousness, spiritual and even physical inertia.

It is the concrete spirit of a people which we must concretely recognize. And because it is spirit, it can only be grasped spiritually, through thought. This is the spirit that sprouts forth in all deeds and tendencies of the people, that brings itself to actualization, to self-enjoyment, and self-knowledge. The highest achievement of the spirit, however, is self-knowledge, not only intuitive but rational cognizance of itself. This it must and also will achieve. But this achievement is at the same time its decline. It is the rise of another spirit, another world-historical people, another epoch of world history. This transition and connection of national spirits lead us to the connection of the whole, to the concept of world history as such, which we must now more closely examine and which we must understand.

(b) THE DIALECTIC OF NATIONAL PRINCIPLES

World history in general is the development of Spirit in *Time,* just as nature is the development of the Idea in *Space.*

When we cast a glance at world history in general, we see a

[9] Here appears clearly the distinction Hegel has in mind throughout between the state as a bureaucratic system of norms and commands, on the one hand, and as the culture of a people, on the other. The former is no bearer of morality, the latter is.

tremendous picture of transformations and actions, an infinite of varied formations of peoples, states, individuals, in restless succession. Everything that can enter and interest the mind of man, every sentiment of goodness, beauty, greatness is called into play. Everywhere aims are adopted and pursued which we recognize, whose accomplishment we desire; we hope and fear for them. In all these events and accidents we see human activity and suffering in the foreground, everywhere something which is part and parcel of ourselves, and therefore everywhere our interest takes sides for or against. At times we are attracted by beauty, freedom, and richness, at others by energy, by which even vice knows how to make itself important. At other times we see the large mass of a universal interest move heavily along, only to be abandoned to and pulverized by an infinite complexity of trifling circumstances. Then again we see trivial results from gigantic expenditures of forces or tremendous results from seemingly insignificant causes. Everywhere the motliest throng which draws us into its circle; when the one disappears, the other swiftly takes its place.

This restless succession of individuals and peoples, who exist for a time and then disappear, presents to us a universal thought, a category: that of *change* in general. To comprehend this change from its negative side, all we have to do is to look at the ruins of past splendor. What traveler has not been moved by the ruins of Carthage, Palmyra, Persepolis, Rome to think of the transitoriness of empires and men, to mourn the passing of once vigorous and flourishing life? This sadness does not dwell on personal loss and the transitoriness of one's own purposes; it is disinterested sadness about the passing of splendid and highly developed human life. But then we pass on to another thought just as intimately connected with the idea of change, the positive fact, namely, that ruin is at the same time emergence of a new life, that out of life arises death, but out of death, life. This is a great thought which the Orientals fully understood and which is the highest thought of their metaphysics. In the conception of the migration of souls it refers to individuals. In the better known image of the *Phoenix*, however, it refers to all natural life, continuously preparing its own pyre and consuming itself so that from its ashes the new, rejuvenated, fresh life continually arises. This picture, however, is Asiatic; oriental, not occidental. The Spirit, devouring its worldly envelope, not only passes into another envelope, not only arises rejuvenated from the ashes of its embodiment, but it emerges from them exalted, transfigured, a purer Spirit. It is true that it acts against itself, devours its own existence. But in so doing it elaborates upon this existence; its embodiment becomes material for its work to elevate itself to a new embodiment.

We must, then, consider the spirit in this respect. Its transformations are not merely rejuvenating transitions, returns to the same form. They are elaborations upon itself, by which it multiplies the material for its endeavors. Thus it experiments in a multitude of dimensions and directions, developing itself, exercising itself, enjoying itself in inexhaustible abundance. For each of its creations, satisfying for the moment, presents new material, a new challenge for further elaboration. The abstract thought of mere change gives place to the thought of Spirit manifesting, developing, and differentiating its powers in all the directions of its plenitude. What powers it possesses in itself we understand by the multiplicity of its products and formations. In this lust of activity it only deals with itself. Though involved with the conditions of nature, both inner and outer, it not only meets in them opposition and hindrance, but often failure and defeat through the complications into which it becomes involved through them or through itself. But even when it perishes it does so in the course of its function and destiny, and even then it offers the spectacle of having proved itself as spiritual activity.

The very essence of spirit is *action*. It makes itself what it essentially is; it is its own product, its own work. Thus it becomes object of itself, thus it is presented to itself as an external existence. Likewise the spirit of a people: it is a definite spirit which builds itself up to an objective world. This world, then, stands and continues in its religion, its cult, its customs, its constitution and political laws, the whole scope of its institutions, its events and deeds. This is its work: this *one* people! Peoples are what their deeds are. Every Englishman will say, we are the ones who navigate the ocean and dominate world commerce, who own East India and its wealth, who have a parliament, juries, and so on. The function of the individual is to appropriate to himself this substantial being, make it part of his character and capacity, and thus to become something in the world. For he finds the existence of the people as a ready-made, stable world, into which he must fit himself. The spirit of the people, then, enjoys and satisfies itself in its work, in its world.

The people is moral, virtuous, strong when it brings forth what it wills. It defends its product against outside powers through the work of its objectification. The tension between (its potentiality and its actuality) what it is in itself, subjectively, in its inner purpose and essence, and what it really is (objectively), is thus abolished. It is with itself (actualized), it has itself objectively before itself. But then this activity of spirit is no longer necessary; it has what it wanted. The people can still do a great deal in war and peace, internally and externally. But the living, substantial soul itself is, so to speak, no longer active. The deepest, highest interest thus has gone out of life; for interest is only where there is opposition. The people lives like an individual passing from manhood to old age, enjoying himself, for he is exactly what he wanted to be and was able to achieve. Even though his imagination may have gone further, it has abandoned more far-reaching purposes; if reality did not fit them, he fits the purposes to reality. It is this life of *habit*—the watch is wound up and goes by itself—which brings about natural death. Habit is tensionless activity. Only formal duration is left to it, in which plenitude and depth of purpose need no longer to be heard. Existence has become, so to speak, external, sensuous; it is not absorbed any more in its purpose. Thus individuals die, thus peoples die a natural death. Although the latter continue in existence, it is an uninterested, lifeless existence; its institutions are without necessity, just because the necessity has been satisfied—all political life is triviality and boredom. If a truly general interest is desired, then the spirit of the people would have to come to the point of wanting something new—but whence this something new? It would be a higher, more universal idea of itself, transcending its present principle; but this, precisely, would manifest the presence of a wider principle, a new spirit.

Such a new principle does indeed come into the spirit of a people which has arrived at its completion and actualization. It not merely dies a natural death, for it is no merely single individual, but has spiritual, universal life. Its natural death appears rather as the killing of itself by itself. The reason for this difference from the single, natural individual is that the national spirit exists as a genus, and consequently carries its own negation within itself, the very universality of its existence. A people can die a violent death only when it has become naturally dead in itself, such as the German Imperial Cities (*Reichsstädte*) or the German Imperial Constitution.[10]

The universal spirit does not merely die a natural death; it does not simply vanish in the senile life of mere habit. Insofar as it is a national spirit and a part of world history itself, it also comes to know its work and to think itself. It is world-historical only insofar as in its fundamental elements, its essential purpose, there is a *universal* principle; only insofar is the work which such a spirit produces a moral, political organization. If it is mere desires which impel peoples to actions, then such actions pass without leaving traces, or rather, its traces are mere corruption and ruin.

Thus at first Cronos ruled, Time itself—the golden age without moral works. What it produced, its children, were

---

[10] Hegel means of course the constitution of the Holy Roman Empire of the German Nation, which expired on August 6, 1806. But what he says also applies to the Imperial Germany which lasted from 1871 to 1918.

devoured by it. Only Zeus, who gave birth to Athene out of his head and whose circle included Apollo and the Muses, conquered Time and set a limit to its lapse. He is the political God, who has produced a moral work, the State.

In work itself is implied the elemental character of universality, of Thought. Without Thought it has no objectivity; thought is its fundamental definition. The highest point of a people's development is the rational consciousness of its life and conditions, the scientific understanding of its laws, its system of justice, its morality. For in this unity (of subjective and objective) lies the most intimate unity in which Spirit can be with itself. The purpose of its work is to have itself as object. But Spirit can have itself as object only by thinking itself.

At this point, then, Spirit knows its principles, the universal element of its actions. But this work of Thought, being universal, is at the same time different in form from the particular, real work, and from the concrete life which brings the work about. When this point is attained, we have both a real and an ideal existence. If (for example) we want to gain a general representation and a concept of the Greeks and their life, we find it in Sophocles and Aristophanes, in Thucydides and Plato. In these individuals the Greek spirit grasped itself in thought and representation. This is its deeper satisfaction (its consummation); but it is at the same time ideal and different from its active reality.

In such a time, a people, therefore, necessarily finds a satisfaction in the idea of virtue. Talk about virtue partly accompanies, partly replaces real virtue. On the other hand, pure universal Thought, being universal, is apt to bring the particular and unreflected—faith, confidence, custom—to reflection about itself and its immediate (simple and unreflected) existence. It thus shows up the limitation of unreflected life, partly by giving it reasons on hand by which to secede from its duties, partly by asking about reasons and the connection with universal thought. Then, in not finding the latter, it tries to shatter duty itself as without foundation.

Therewith [11] appears the isolation of the individuals from each other and the whole, their aggressive selfishness and vanity, their seeking of advantage and satisfaction at the expense of the whole. For the inward principle of such isolation (not only produces the content but) the *form* of subjectivity—selfishness and corruption in the unbound passions and egotistic interests of men.

Thus Zeus and his race were themselves devoured, Zeus who set an end to the devouring action of Time and stayed this transiency by firmly establishing something lasting in itself. He was devoured by the generative agent, namely, the principle of Thought, of knowledge, of reasoning, of insight from and demand for reasons.[12]

Time is the negative element in the sensuous world. Thought is the same negativity, but its deepest, its infinite form. It therefore resolves all existence in general, but first in its finite, its definite form. For existence in general is determined as objective.[13] It therefore appears as given and immediate, as authority. It is finite and limited either as content or (as form; the latter) as the bound for the thinking subject and its infinite reflection in itself.

[*The resolution of existence through thought is at the same time necessarily the arising of a new principle. Thought as universal is resolving, but this resolution actually contains the preceding principle within it, though no longer in its original form but transfigured through universality.*] Thus life emerges out of death; but it is only individual life. If we consider the genus as the substantial in this transformation, then the death of the individual is a falling back of the genus into individuality. The preservation of the genus is then nothing but the monotonous repetition of the same kind of existence.

---

[11] With the disintegration of the intuitive bonds of society—faith, confidence, custom.

[12] Which abolished the gods. (On the other hand, Reason makes out of the chronological sequence of history a logical sequence and this, in excising Time out of history, to a certain degree vindicates Zeus.)

[13] See above, pp. 32ff.

Cognition, the thinking comprehension of being, is the source and birthplace of a new spiritual form, a higher form, whose principle is partly preserving, partly transfiguring its material. For Thought is the universal, the genus which is immortal and preserves its identity. The particular form of Spirit not only passes away naturally in time, but is abolished through the self-acting, self-mirroring activity of self-consciousness. Since this abolition is activity of Thought, it is both preservation and transfiguration. While thus Spirit, on the one hand, abolishes the actuality, the subsistence of what it is, on the other hand, it gains thereby the essence, the Thought, the universal of that which it *only was* (of its transient condition). Its principle is no longer this immediate content and purpose of what it previously was, but the essence of it.

The result of this process, then, is that the Spirit in objectifying itself and thinking its own being, on the one hand, destroys this (particular) determination of its own being and, on the other hand, grasps its universality. It thus gives a new determination to its principle. The substantial determination of this national spirit is therewith changed; its principle passes into a new and higher one.

It is most important for the full understanding and comprehension of history to grasp and possess the thought of this transition. An individual as unity traverses various stages and remains the same individual. So also a people, up to the stage which is the universal stage of its spirit. In this consists the inner, the conceptual necessity of its change. Here we have the essence, the very soul of the philosophical understanding of history.

Spirit is essentially the result of its own activity. Its activity is transcending the immediately given, negating it, and returning into itself. We can compare it with the seed of a plant, which is both beginning and result of the plant's whole life. The powerlessness of life manifests itself precisely in this falling apart of beginning and end. Likewise in the lives of individuals and peoples. The life of a people brings a fruit to maturity, for its activity aims at actualizing its principle.

But the fruit does not fall back into the womb of the people which has produced and matured it. On the contrary, it turns into a bitter drink for this people. The people cannot abandon it, for it has an unquenchable thirst for it. But imbibing the drink is the drinker's destruction, yet, at the same time the rise of a new principle.

We have already seen what the final purpose of this process is. The principles of the national spirits progressing through a necessary succession of stages are only moments of the one universal Spirit which through them elevates and completes itself into a self-comprehending *totality*.

Thus, in dealing with the idea of Spirit only and in considering the whole of world history as nothing but its manifestation, we are dealing only with the *present*—however long the past may be which we survey. [*There is no time where it (the Spirit) has not been nor will not be; it neither was nor is it yet to be. It is forever* now.] The Idea is ever present, the Spirit immortal. [*What is true is eternal in and for itself, neither yesterday nor tomorrow but* now *in the sense of absolute presence. In the Idea, what may seem lost is eternally preserved.*] This implies that the present stage of Spirit contains all previous stages within itself. These, to be sure, have unfolded themselves successively and separately, but Spirit still is what it has in itself always been. The differentiation of its stages is but the development of what it is in itself. The life of the ever-present Spirit is a cycle of stages, which, on the one hand, co-exist side by side, but, on the other hand, seem to be past. The moments which Spirit seems to have left behind, it still possesses in the depth of its present.

The Library of Liberal Arts

Below is a representative selection from The Library of Liberal Arts. This partial listing—taken from the more than 200 scholarly editions of the world's finest literature and philosophy—indicates the scope, nature, and concept of this distinguished series.